October 1975

To the memory of Clyde R. Payne,
our grandpa, who was Hometown U.S.A.
With love
Sherry Payne Voelling, Karan Payne Miller

HOMETOWN

U.S.A.

Stephen W. Sears

Murray Belsky

Douglas Tunstell

Published by AMERICAN HERITAGE PUBLISHING CO., INC., New York
Book Trade Distribution by SIMON AND SCHUSTER

HOMETOWN U.S.A.

Stephen W. Sears *Editor/Author*

Murray Belsky *Art Director*

Douglas Tunstell *Picture Editor*

Brenda Savard *Copy Editor*

Mary Elizabeth Wise *Researcher*

AMERICAN HERITAGE PUBLISHING CO., INC.

Paul Gottlieb, *President and Publisher*

Kenneth W. Leish, *General Manager, Book Division*

Murray Belsky, *Editorial Art Director*

Copyright © 1975 by American Heritage Publishing Co., Inc., a subsidiary of McGraw-Hill, Inc., 1221 Avenue of the Americas, New York, N.Y. 10020. All rights reserved. Printed in the United States of America. No part of this publication may be reproduced, stored in a retrieval system, or transmitted, in any form or by any means, electronic, mechanical, photocopying, recording, or otherwise, without the prior written permission of the publisher.

Library of Congress Cataloging in Publication Data: page 224
ISBN: 671-22079-9

These good citizens of Corning, New York, enjoying themselves on a winter afternoon were photographed about 1905 by Isabel Walker Drake, using a wide-angle panoramic camera. The charmer on the half-title page, all dressed up and ready to travel, was also photographed by Mrs. Drake; the scene is the family's summer place on Keuka Lake, New York, and the date is July, 1912. The photograph on the title page depicts the circus, led by a bandwagon, parading down the main street of Newton, New Jersey, about 1910. It is from Brown Brothers; the other two are from the American Heritage Collection.

Introduction	6
1 Main Street	10
2 All Around the Town	42
3 Home and Family	76
4 Growing Up	110
5 Life's Small Pleasures	146
6 Remembered Moments	192
Acknowledgments	224

Hartford Public Library
Croton, Ohio

Introduction

This book is about a way of life that no longer exists. It disappeared from the American landscape more than a half-century ago, about the time of the Great War. A coroner might list the cause of death as the automobile, but an autopsy would reveal additional fatal symptoms running as deep as the wholesale realignment of the nation's economic and social structures then taking place. Yet over the life of a generation or two, from about 1880 to the First World War, this way of life reached its apogee, and it has left a permanent imprint on our national character.

Hometown U.S.A. is about small-town America—what it looked like, what it felt like to live there—in an era whose midpoint was the turn of the century. "It is the small town, the small city, that is our heredity," wrote the distinguished editor and critic Henry Seidel Canby in *The Age of Confidence* in 1934; "we have made twentieth-century America from it, and some account of those communities as they were . . . we owe to our children and grandchildren." We concur, and offer here our own account, built around of-the-period photographs, of what is the spiritual if not the actual hometown of modern-day Americans.

Links with that time are intact. Those among us in their mid-sixties and older have memories of growing up then. Many of the rest of us possess reminiscences and memorabilia—letters, clippings, dog-eared family picture albums—from the period, handed down by parents or grandparents. Not all these direct and indirect experiences of an earlier day deal with small-town life, of course, but the percentage that do may seem surprisingly large to today's heavily urbanized and suburbanized society. The census of 1900 reported that 22 per cent of America's 76 million people lived in hamlets, villages, towns, and fledgling cities that ranged in population from a few score to 25,000. Nearly 40 million people were described by the census as living in "rural territory," and for them the nearest country town was mecca, the place where they bought their supplies, sold their produce, and learned their news. Thus three-quarters of the nation's population at the turn of the century had more than a nodding acquaintance with small-town living.

The 1900 census also counted no fewer than 10,508 communities across the nation with populations under 25,000. Our sampling of that number is inevitably a small one, but its range is wide geographically and by type. In these pages will be found people and scenes photographed in country towns and industrial towns, new towns and old towns, big towns and small towns.

All of them may be defined as "settled-in" places, where basic small-town institutions had appeared and family life had taken root (excluded, for example, are raw Western mining camps). The smallest community pictured is Merna, Nebraska, with a population in 1900 of 141. One or two others are in the 25,000 range, which technically makes them small cities. However, we have caught these places in mid-flight, so to speak; experiencing rapid growth to small-city status, they had not yet outdistanced their small-town characteristics.

Our primary resource has been the small-town commercial photographer. The number of men and women in that profession was surprisingly large; of a nationwide total of 31,775 photographers listed in the 1910 census, more than half, 16,700, were based in small towns. Their beat was succinctly described in an advertisement placed by L.E. Lindsay and J.L.B. Smith, partners who worked out of Nashau, New Hampshire. The Lindsay & Smith studio assured the public that it was prepared to produce "Views of Homesteads, Interiors, Public Buildings, Family Gatherings, School Classes and Groups, taken to order on short notice." Most such photographers found it necessary to roam beyond their home base to generate enough business to support themselves. Theodore Teeple, for example, maintained galleries in Ashland, Wooster, and Massillon, Ohio, requiring him to journey some 50 miles to cover all three. The Howes brothers of Ashfield, Massachusetts, were even more itinerant, spending their entire summers crisscrossing the Connecticut Valley by horse and buggy from Hartford nearly to the Vermont border to pick up commissions.

John Runk, the operator of the American Eagle Studio in Stillwater, Minnesota, was typical of the breed. A friend took the overleaf picture of him at work early in the century. Runk was 21 when he opened for business as a photographer in Stillwater in the last year of the old century, and photography remained his avocation for the rest of his 86 years. As his picture of celebrating the Armistice (pages 192-193) demonstrates, he took an active part in the community. He also possessed a sense of history and sought to assemble a photographic record of the surrounding area, his beloved St. Croix Valley. He willed what he described as his "historical collection" to the Minnesota Historical Society.

John Runk had the foresight to see to the preservation of his collection, but most small-town photographers did not or could not. A good many of them continued to work with glass-plate negatives long after flexible film came into use, either because they were used to working that way or because they preferred the clarity and depth of the image on glass. Consequently, while the quality of what has survived from the period is often exceptional, the problem of survival was intensified. The pictorial record on glass that J.J. Pennell made of Junction City, Kansas, over the course of 35 years weighed some four tons. Fortunately, after Pennell's death in 1922 his son preserved the plates and eventually presented them to the University of Kansas. Similarly, an even larger collection of glass negatives taken in Cooperstown, New York, by Arthur "Putt" Telfer was rescued from destruction by the New York State Historical Association. (Telfer was very much the traditionalist, continuing to make glass negatives well into the 1930's and continuing to drive his 1916 Model T until his death in 1954, at age 95.) Paul Vanderbilt, so instrumental in building the superb photographic collection at the State Historical Society of Wisconsin, had an uncanny talent for sniffing out caches of dusty glass plates. There are many similar stories of concerned laymen or dedicated curators rescuing collections of old pictures—sometimes literally from the town dump. But how many thousands upon thousands of the fragile glass negatives have disintegrated or been broken or simply thrown away by the unthinking can only be guessed.

To these commercial photographers, there was nothing very special about most of their assignments. It was part of regular business routine to take a portrait or to photograph a wedding group, a merchant posing proudly with his wares, or a traveling carnival setting up in Main Street. Beyond using whatever natural skill in composition and tact for handling subjects that they possessed, the professional photographers represented in this book were not setting out to produce a personal artistic statement. (One exception is Belle Johnson of Monroe City, Missouri, who in her spare time liked to experiment with what she called her character studies; we could not resist using two of them—pages 88 and 120 —for they reflect more artless charm than deliberate artistry.) It is this quality of unself-consciousness that gives these pictures their candor and their historical value. Since neither the subjects nor the photographers were striving for effect, what emerges is simply good reporting, and the reward of patient study and analysis of these old pictures is a heightened understanding of another time and another place.

A substantial number of pictures made by talented amateurs will also be found on these pages. For some, photography was a hobby that led them to experiment with a variety of cameras and materials; for others, the fun was less in the technique than in the subject matter. Mrs. Jeanette Bernard seems to have been in the latter category. She is shown below right, photographed posing a young family member or friend. Most of what can be said about Mrs. Bernard has to be deduced from her pictures. We are certain only that she lived in a quiet community somewhere in the borough of Queens on New York's Long Island. "On the outskirts of the city, life was much like that in a country village," writes John A. Kouwenhoven of Mrs. Bernard's milieu at the turn of the century. Nearly all of her pictures were taken in or around her home—in the kitchen, on the back porch, in the yard by the grape arbor, in a nearby wooded area—and they present a view of the household domestic scene that is almost unique for this period. Commercial photographers rarely had cause to take pictures of such "ordinary" scenes, and so our visual record is dependent on amateurs like Mrs. Bernard who had the wit—and the talent—to make the everyday interesting. (The Bernard Collection is yet another example of a last-minute rescue. Before World War II, D. Jay Culver, the late proprietor of Culver Pictures, acquired her glass-plate negatives from a New York dealer in old glass.)

Inasmuch as all these photographs are eyewitness documentation of an era, the chapter introductions and picture commentaries that accompany them also utilize eyewitness testimony. The memoirists and commentators quoted grew up around the turn of the century, and their observations about the small town and its institutions, and what childhood there was like, are sharp and clear, undimmed by time and distance; obviously, the small town's impact on them was strong.

The three or four decades that center on the turn of the century are popularly considered the heart and soul of the Good Old Days. It is a term used with derision as well as approbation. In truth, it was a highly complex period. For the recent immigrant huddled in New York's Hell's Kitchen or Chicago's Little Poland, for anyone sunk in the urban masses, these were not golden years. Life on the more isolated farms remained an endless routine of hard labor, loneliness, and continuous gambling with nature. This is the theme of Otto L. Bettmann's recent book uncompromisingly titled *The Good Old Days—They Were Terrible!* What is presented by the uncritically nostalgic, he complains, "is a glowing picture of the past, of blue-skied meadows where children play and millionaires sip tea."

Bettmann deals primarily with the urban scene, especially New York City, but what of the scene in America's small towns? Certainly, life there was not idyllic. There can be no doubt that the everyday routine of living was considerably more demanding in 1900 than is true of the 1970's. Illness and epidemics were distressingly common, medical care and public health services distressingly inadequate. For the working man, whether he clerked in the general store or labored in the carriage shop on the edge of town, hours were long, pay low, and benefits non-existent. His wife ran a household without machinery and conveniences now taken for granted, doing everything laboriously by hand from scrubbing clothes with homemade soap on Monday morning to singeing the chicken for Sunday's dinner. It is difficult to work up much nostalgic longing for an outdoor privy on a January morning or the plagues of flies

MINNESOTA HISTORICAL SOCIETY

Town photographer John Runk of Stillwater, Minnesota.

endemic to a horse-drawn society. As Sinclair Lewis in *Main Street* led the way in pointing out, there was often a shortage of intellectual stimulation in the Gopher Prairies of America; narrowness, bigotry, dullness, and limited opportunity were common enough to push many a youth out into the wider world.

When all this is said, however, there remain certain appealing and enduring qualities about small-town living not easily forgotten by those who left as well as by those who stayed. Even Sinclair Lewis, according to biographer Mark Schorer, believed in his "other moods" the small town "to be the best place after all, the real America, America at the roots, America at its kindest, its friendliest, its human best."

The friendliness and kindness are taken almost for granted in the remembered vignettes: the summer evening strolls under the elms or the live oaks with stops to chat with neighbors rocking on their front porches; the blacksmith's cheerful tolerance of small boys who rooted around the forge for stray bits of iron; the bonhomie of the barbershop; the gossip traded over the back fence. This is the mood so prevalent in Thornton Wilder's celebrated play *Our Town*, written, Wilder said, "out of a deep admiration for those little white towns in the hills. . . ."; in Grover's Corners he hoped "to find value above all price for the smallest events in our daily life."

There was also a special mood that enveloped many Americans, especially small-town Americans, in this era that Canby termed the Age of Confidence. They "really believed all they heard on the Fourth of July or read in school readers," he wrote. "They set on one plane of time, and that the present, the Declaration of Independence, the manifest destiny of America, the new plumbing, the growth of the factory system, the morning paper, and the church sociable. It was all there at once, better than elsewhere, their own, and permanent. . . . They had just the country they wanted . . . and they believed it would be the same, except for more bathtubs and faster trains, forever. . . ." And he concludes, "for the last time in living memory everyone knew exactly what it meant to be an American."

One more characteristic of the time and place may be mentioned—a simplicity and directness to life that has become exceedingly rare in this complex, faster-paced era. "We concede to natural activities, honest materials, and simple pleasures a poetic possibility that we do not find in mechanized entertainment and mass-produced gadgets," Wallace Stegner has observed. There is an imprint upon us today, he adds, a "homesickness that encloses local history as bark encloses a tree. And homesickness . . . not simply for a place, but for a time, a tempo, a way of thinking and working and being, a way of associating with other people and with the natural world."

"Most of that life is gone, extinct as the dodo bird," novelist Conrad Richter wrote. It is probably true that figments of wishful thinking have embellished the Good Old Days; still, if they ever did exist, if they marked a time when tranquility, individuality, decency, and peace of mind were the common currency of daily living —when, as Richter put it, the chief product of life was joy rather than ease—then one place they were surely found was in the small towns of America seven or eight decades ago.
—Stephen W. Sears

Amateur photographer Mrs. Jeanette Bernard and friend.

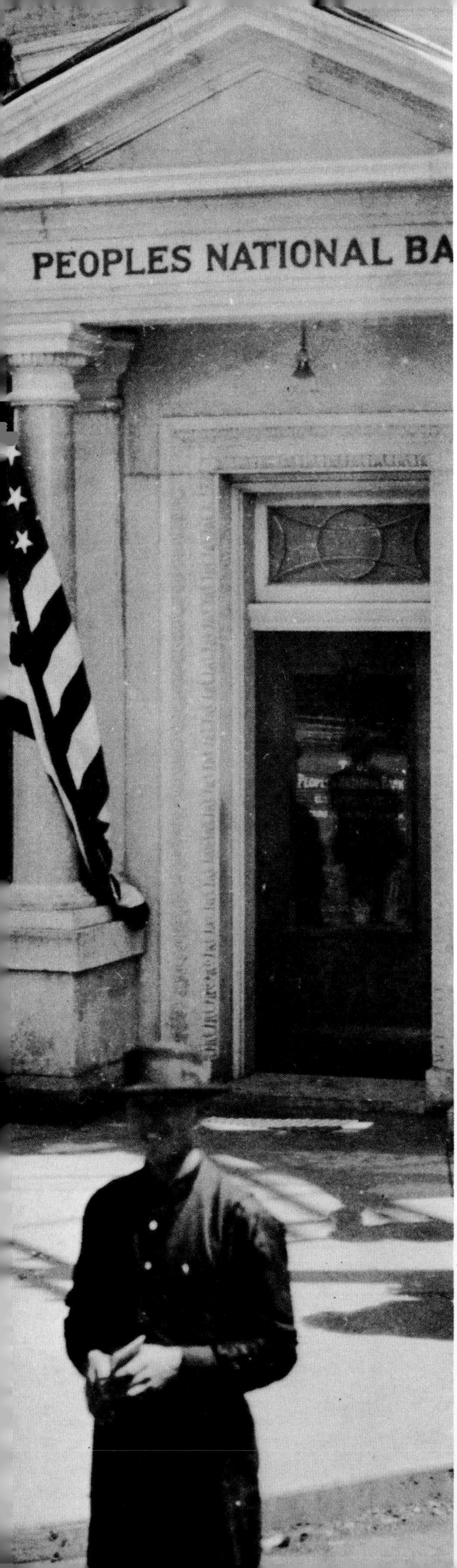

BANDHOLTZ COLLECTION, LIBRARY OF CONGRESS

CHAPTER

1
Main Street

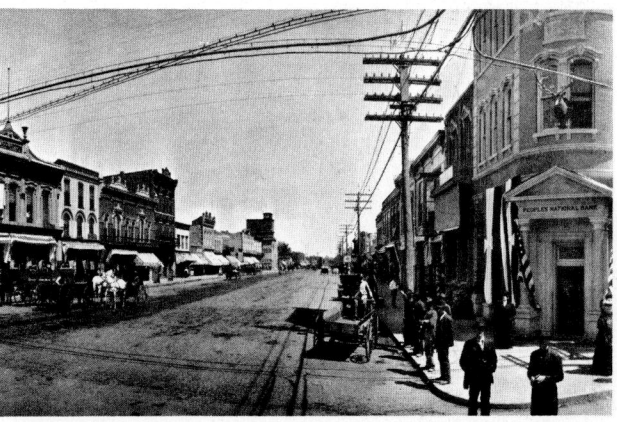

It cannot be stated with assurance how many Main Streets there have been in the United States, but certainly the number is in the hundreds. At left is a close-up view of one of them: Main Street in Ottawa, Kansas, photographed in 1909 by the panoramist Fred Bandholtz (page 17). It is a detail of the larger scene reproduced above.

Ottawa was a not inconsiderable town in 1909. A county seat, a producer of soap, flour, furniture, and carriages, served by two railroads, it was home to 7,600 people. Planted firmly on the corner of Main and Second was the Peoples National Bank, with the Dickey and Porter land office upstairs; the elk's head that graced Dickey and Porter's front windows (above) had its antlers tipped with light bulbs and must have been a 24-hour attraction. Among the bank's near neighbors were a barbershop, a music store, and a millinery. By all appearances, Ottawa was a town entirely typical of its time and place: buildings more sturdy than architecturally distinguished, the horse comfortably co-existing with the few motorcars in town, and no one outside without a hat.

This opening chapter offers a modest Grand Tour of Main Street—or Elm Street or Fifth Avenue or whatever a town's main stem was called—as it looked three-quarters of a century ago. The typical Main Street, comfortably wide enough to allow teams to turn, was packed dirt (although by 1910 brick or other paving was becoming common). Dust, mud, and slush in season and horse droppings at all times required pedestrians to tread carefully. Hitching posts and watering troughs—today's parking meters and gas stations—were conveniently located. In the early days, rather than sidewalks stores commonly had raised platforms out front for the convenience of customers loading their wagons, but in more flourishing towns the practice was abandoned out of consideration for pedestrian traffic. Another sign of the modern age was the overhead tangle of electric and telephone wires. In some of these pictures street signs can be detected, but many towns did not bother with such frills; if you didn't know where you were, went the reasoning, you shouldn't be there.

Geographically these scenes range from Stillwater, Minnesota, to Jackson, Mississippi, and from Milford, New Hampshire, to Socorro in New Mexico Territory, yet they suggest a certain universality about small-town America in that era. Drugstore interiors, say, or the front window displays of hardwares varied hardly at all from coast to coast and from border to border. Some were more elaborate and carried more stock or were lighted with electricity rather than kerosene, but it is safe to say that the Main Street "fixtures" on the following pages represent a national cross section.

This is not surprising, for their offerings were limited (by today's standards) and essentially uniform. The great majority of American small-town dwellers in this period were of the working class. They were chronically short of cash and out of necessity did for themselves whenever they could. Conspicuous consumption was limited to the mill owner or the banker up on the hill—if it was even practiced there. Consequently, purchases were made from limited stock and confined mostly to meeting simple, universal needs. The organized jumble of the general store, for example, would have been immediately comprehensible to any newcomer in town, and a horse being a horse, the smithy in Boylston, Massachusetts (pages 30–31), could not have looked very different from the smithy in Boylston, Indiana.

As seen in this chapter and subsequent ones, there was definite regional diversity in the American small-town landscape, but where it was most evident was in a town's over-all look. White clapboard and spreading elms shading the green bespoke New England, just as adobe and false fronts characterized the Southwest. Stolid brick trimmed with stone and cast-iron gingerbread became a Midwestern Main Street staple. (It may be supposed that Mr. Bandholtz, who took the view on the previous pages and the one on pages 16–17 and scores of others like them across Iowa and Kansas and Nebraska, grew weary indeed of peering through his ground glass at what must have looked each time like the same town.)

Even the shortest and muddiest Main Street had its minimum complement of commercial establishments. Most important was the general store, which carried, as one proprietor claimed, "Almost Everything," and often doubled as the town's post office. Another essential was the drugstore, where patent medicines made up the largest single class of merchandise and where the soda fountain was one of the most popular spots in town. Often there was a bank, which, whatever its true condition, at least *looked* solvent and substantial. There might be a hardware, offering a line almost as varied as the general store; a hotel, offering accommodations and front-porch sitting space to the traveling man; and a barbershop, offering gossip, bay rum, and the *Police Gazette*. If local option permitted, there was usually a saloon, and farther out Main Street might be found the butcher, the livery stable, and the blacksmith. If the town had railroad service (and every self-respecting town coveted it during that golden age of railroading), there was a depot and freight office.

As a town experienced growth and prosperity, Main Street's services grew in number and specialization. The druggist and barber and saloonkeeper found themselves with competitors. The functions of the general store were split up. The grocery and the fruit and vegetable store displayed fresh produce out front under striped awnings, and women shoppers could find dry goods and notions under one roof and millinery under another. Restaurants, "elegant ice cream rooms," cigar stores, booteries, clothiers, jewelers—and photographers—set up shop. The opera house provided a hall for any occasion, and the weekly newspaper furnished a sense of community. Schools, churches, and other touches of civilization might also be seen along Main Street, but usually (as in Fountain City, Wisconsin, pictured overleaf) they stood apart from the commercial district. This was also generally the case with grain elevators, mills, and industrial units of various sorts. Finally Main Street was paved and trolley tracks were laid and a small town was on its way to becoming a small city.

Of course, there were any number of Main Streets that experienced no such growth. Some lost economic lifeblood and faded away. Others remained at the wide-spot-in-the-road, general store-and-drugstore stage. Still others reached the plateau of specialization suggested in these pictures and stabilized there. Fountain City had a population of 1,031 when the picture overleaf was taken; seven decades later, 1,017 people lived there.

Virtually every memoirist and commentator on small-town life has retained vivid memories of Main Street fixtures. William Allen White recalled with fondness his father's drugstore in Eldorado, Kansas, especially the great bottles of colored water "shining red or blue or green" in the window and the soda fountain "with half a dozen flavors—lemon, strawberry, banana, raspberry and 'don't care,' which was a mixture of the odds and ends of all of them." Louis Bromfield could remember every detail of the livery stables in his hometown of Mansfield, Ohio: the whiskey, card games, and lurid gossip retailed at Painter's, and the "gentlemen horses" kept at stud at Grimses', much to the outrage of local mothers intent on protecting the innocence of their young charges. Bromfield was convinced that a boy's sex education was better acquired at the livery than at the Y.M.C.A.

Paul M. Angle, the Lincoln scholar, also grew up in Mansfield, and at the age of nine he was impressed to serve in his father's grocery. The rewards of the job included the freshest Golden Bantam short of the field, clandestine tidbits of a tasty summer sausage called "Lebanon bologna," the exciting arrival of big bamboo-bound containers of tea from the mysterious East, and the multiple pleasures of the annual grocers' picnic at Cedar Point amusement park on Lake Erie. But a good deal of hard work was required of him as well, particularly the manhandling of large wheels of cheese and tubs of salt mackerel and barrels of vinegar. There was also endless labor with balance-scales and scoops and paper bags. In the time before cellophane and polyethylene seized control, Angle's grocery maintained a refreshing merchandising policy. "Selling bulk goods," Angle writes, "was trade practice, but with my father it was also the result of a strong conviction. Bulk goods, he believed—and with reason—were just as good as those that came already packaged, and always cheaper. Why make the customer pay an unnecessary premium?"

Nothing stirs a memoirist's nostalgia more vigorously than recollections of the old general store, and no one has chronicled this American institution more lovingly than Gerald Carson. When one entered those double doors, Carson writes, "there was a sense of the world's good things in limitless profusion, long counters down either side, with rounded glass showcases spaced along on top of the counters, the whole length of the side walls lined with drawers, bins and shelves. . . ." Not all the lasting impressions were visual: "There was a fragrance which still stands out in memory above all else. Perhaps it was not exactly a fragrance, but more of an aroma, mellow and substantial. . . . All diarists and old-timers agree that it was a well-dug-in odor, with lots of authority, a blend made up of the store's inventory, the customers and the cat. Identifiable still, down memory's lane, are the contributions of ripe cheese and sauerkraut, sweet pickles, the smell of bright paint on new toys, kerosene, lard and molasses, old onions and potatoes, poultry feed, gun oil, rubber boots, calico, dried fish, coffee, . . . and tobacco smoke."

Christmas time was a special time at the general store. In addition to augmenting the candy display—which already included "jawbreakers, cinnamon red hots, 'lickerish' shoe strings, bellyburners, one cent each; and glorious Zanzibars, either lemon or peppermint-flavored, that kept fresh through all weather and in all climates"; and a dozen other varieties—hardware supplies were pushed back into the stock room to make space for "toys, watches, tiny knives and forks, wooden soldiers, dolls with china heads and kidskin bodies, [and] linen dogs and cats, to be stuffed and sewed up at home. . . . Articles of the omnipresent 'tin' made a brave show." December was traditionally the month when the steady customer settled up his account ("Short settlements," advised *Willard's Almanac*, "make long friends"), and when that was done the storekeeper customarily acknowledged the transaction by passing out a good five-cent cigar, adding to the conviviality of the season.

The pictures in this chapter present the independent small-town merchant in his heyday. Most of them were taken by local photographers, who were commissioned to portray the merchant at his post, very much his own boss and obviously proud of the fact. In none of these scenes is there any sign of a chain store or other interstate retailer. (They were lurking just offstage, however. In 1900 A & P's sales topped $5 million, Woolworth's had 59 stores, and there was even a cigar-store chain that was putting up signs warning "No loafing—all room needed for business".)

Sweeping changes might well be in the offing, but for the moment a cigar store like Mosier's (page 28) still considered loafing space and a wooden Indian good for business, Breckel's (page 19) encouraged customers to sniff and otherwise closely inspect the fruit, and the aroma in Arkalon's general store (pages 20–21) was surely exactly as Gerald Carson remembered.

In the late 1890's Gerhard Gesell climbed Eagle Bluff to capture the largest part of Fountain City, Wisconsin, on a single glass plate—and captured the prototype American small town of the period. Main Street (right center) and Lower Street (far right) mark the commercial area; at the landing are two Mississippi stern-wheelers. Along Hill Street at left is City Hall and the high school (white towers) and two churches. Most back yards in Fountain City contained gardens as well as outhouses and woodsheds.

BANDHOLTZ COLLECTION, LIBRARY OF CONGRESS

Few photographers saw more small-town Main Streets than Fred J. Bandholtz of Des Moines, Iowa, who between 1907 and 1910 earned a living taking panoramic views of the principal intersections of more than a hundred Midwestern towns. This section of a Bandholtz panorama shows Fifth Avenue in Atchison, Kansas, as it looked in 1909. A railroad and shipping center of some 16,000 on the Missouri River, Atchison radiates prosperity: paved streets, storm drains, trolley lines, solid ranks of businesses in brick Gothic. At the left is a popcorn wagon; Moyer's, at the right, is a drugstore.

COLLECTION OF MELVIN ADELGLASS

STATE HISTORICAL SOCIETY OF WISCONSIN

Virtually every businessman along Main Street sooner or later called in the town photographer, who posed him at the front door amidst his employees and samples of his wares. Smith & Strebel's hardware was located in Monroe, New York, Rau's furniture, undertaking, and wallpaper establishment in Beloit, Wisconsin. (The linking of furniture and undertaking grew out of the cabinetmaker's talent for building coffins.) Of Rosenkranse's bootery we know nothing beyond the wide range of its stock. Everyone at Breckel's fruit and vegetable store in Massillon, Ohio, is identified as a Breckel (including the dog, Fritz) except for the "Hon. Robert Folger" in the plug hat.

In *Our Town* one of Thornton Wilder's characters observes that everyone in Grover's Corners looked in daily at the general store and the drugstore. That was also probably the case in Arkalon and Lawrence, Kansas. Arkalon's general store (above) was in the classic mold: dry goods section on the right, with shelves of yard goods and ready-mades and the cabinet of Clark's O.N.T. (Our New Thread); grocery section on the left, with barrels of flour and sugar and crackers, glass cases for cigars and penny candy, and a good array of cans, kegs, bottles, boxes, and bins. At the center of things is the potbellied stove, with chairs and a spittoon for the loungers. The clerks in Raymond's drugstore in Lawrence hammed it up at the soda fountain for the photographer in 1898. At Raymond's the fruit flavors were dispensed with a flourish at a papier-mâché grotto. The extensive collection of patent medicines on the shelves includes Dr. Pierce's Golden Medical Discovery, "the ideal spring tonic and blood purifier."

OVERLEAF: It was a big day at the meat market in Socorro, a town of about a thousand on the Rio Grande in New Mexico Territory, when photographer Joseph E. Smith came to take a business "portrait." These are probably the co-owners, one tidied up in a clean apron, the other taking his ease among the office ledgers. There is fresh sawdust on the floor and the impressive array of carcasses has been carefully arranged and decorated with flags. Such bounty was not normally available in towns of this size, but Socorro was in the heart of good sheep and cattle country. Smith turned to photography in the mid-1880's (he took this in 1886) after trying cowboying and mining.

COLLECTION OF DAVID R. PHILLIPS

BOTH: KANSAS STATE HISTORICAL SOCIETY

A Main Street fixture—except in areas where the W.C.T.U. had gained the upper hand—was the saloon, one of several males-only sanctuaries (the livery and the barbershop were two others) in town. The example at left, in Canandaigua, New York, included not only a well-stocked bar but a quick lunch featuring "Oysters in Every Style" in the back room. In honor of the holidays whiskey was selling for a dollar a quart. The indistinct object on the floor at the right is the bar cat, which moved during the taking of this "flashlight picture." Floyd W. Gunnison, the town photographer, recorded the scene about 1910. The restaurant above, in Stillwater, Minnesota, was photographed that same year by John Runk. Compared to the Canandaigua saloon's busy decor, this place was purely utilitarian, from the bare light bulbs to the nearly bare walls. The lone touch of class was furnished by the intricate and elegant cast iron of the counter stools.

Women had their own sanctuaries, two of which are portrayed here. Opposite is the Pegues-Wright dry goods emporium in Junction City, Kansas, photographed in 1906 by J. J. Pennell. As befitted a town of over 5,300, Pegues-Wright was a good-sized establishment (this is a detail from a view of the full interior) and a well-stocked one, with such innovations as baskets whisked about on overhead trolleys for change-making and package-wrapping; and steam radiators (under the table at left center). This section of the store featured ladies' notions and an assortment of dress goods that ranged from calico at 6 cents a yard to silk at 50 cents. (A sewing machine could be ordered that year from Sears, Roebuck for $12 to $15.) Nearly every town had its millinery shop, where trying on delicate and complicated creations like those seen below was an entirely satisfactory experience. The shop was photographed in Watertown, Wisconsin, by Henry Bergman.

WASHINGTON COUNTY HISTORICAL SOCIETY AND MINNESOTA HISTORICAL SOCIETY

Byron Mosier's cigar store, at the busy corner of Main and Chestnut, and Luke Doyle's barbershop down Chestnut a ways, were two of the landmarks of Stillwater, Minnesota. The barbershop was photographed in 1893, the cigar store in 1910. Barber Doyle (with the mustache), who offered three chairs and no waiting, most likely charged 25 cents for a haircut. In the window of Long John's saloon next to Doyle's is a schedule handbill for the Minneapolis entry in the old Western League, forerunner of the American League. Mr. Mosier marketed his own private-label Byron pipe in addition to advertising a full line of cigars, snuff, and fine-cut. Out front he also displayed a truly splendid example of that unique American art form, the cigar-store Indian.

SOLOMON D. BUTCHER COLLECTION, NEBRASKA STATE HISTORICAL SOCIETY

The horse was still king at the turn of the century, and every town accommodated to that fact. A good blacksmith was always in demand; the artisan at right is shown at work in Boylston, Massachusetts, in 1897. An equally familiar sight was the livery stable; Forney's (above), which served the village of Merna, Nebraska, was photographed in 1904 by Solomon Butcher. Among the livery's functions was supplying horses and rigs to visiting drummers or the town doctor, and for such special occasions as weddings and funerals. It was also where the loafers gathered to gossip and tell the latest traveling salesman story, and thus exercised a strong educative influence on small boys.

OVERLEAF: It took a good-sized and growing town to support a business operation as elaborate as this one. About 1910 Hiram Kernigan Hardy of Jackson, Mississippi, arranged all his rolling stock (hearses at left, ambulances and an "invalid carriage" at right) outside his funeral establishment for photographer Albert Fred Daniel. That is probably Mr. Hardy himself standing at center alongside his new Velie. Why the manhole cover is off remains a mystery.

COLLECTION OF AL FRED DANIEL

SOLOMON D. BUTCHER COLLECTION, NEBRASKA STATE HISTORICAL SOCIETY

The horse was still king at the turn of the century, and every town accommodated to that fact. A good blacksmith was always in demand; the artisan at right is shown at work in Boylston, Massachusetts, in 1897. An equally familiar sight was the livery stable; Forney's (above), which served the village of Merna, Nebraska, was photographed in 1904 by Solomon Butcher. Among the livery's functions was supplying horses and rigs to visiting drummers or the town doctor, and for such special occasions as weddings and funerals. It was also where the loafers gathered to gossip and tell the latest traveling salesman story, and thus exercised a strong educative influence on small boys.

OVERLEAF: It took a good-sized and growing town to support a business operation as elaborate as this one. About 1910 Hiram Kernigan Hardy of Jackson, Mississippi, arranged all his rolling stock (hearses at left, ambulances and an "invalid carriage" at right) outside his funeral establishment for photographer Albert Fred Daniel. That is probably Mr. Hardy himself standing at center alongside his new Velie. Why the manhole cover is off remains a mystery.

COLLECTION OF AL FRED DANIEL

30

300
H. K. HARDY
WALL PAPER
H.K.HARDY
& SIGN PAINTER.
INVALID CARRIAGE

COMMERCIAL NATIONAL BANK
H.O. CAVERT
FARM & CITY PROPERTY
19
03
COMMERCIAL
NATIONAL BANK
U.S. DEPOSITARY

The typical "respectable element" in town, according
to the memoirists, was more often than not headed
by a banker like "our Mr. Brinker, who [as recalled
by Henry Seidel Canby] propelled his crab legs
at nine o'clock every morning down Market Street to the
bank, his mean little eyes swinging right and left
over his scraggly beard. He was a good business man,
and reasonably honest, and constitutionally
incapable of a magnanimous action." There is no
evidence that the commanders of the banks shown here
were anything like Mr. Brinker, but the image has
become a cliché. The Commercial National Bank (left) in
Independence, Kansas, was photographed about 1910;
real-estate agent H. O. Cavert relaxes with a newspaper
in his office upstairs. The 1905 view above,
unveiling the behind-the-counter mysteries of the
First National Bank of Cooperstown, New York,
was taken by town photographer Arthur "Putt" Telfer.

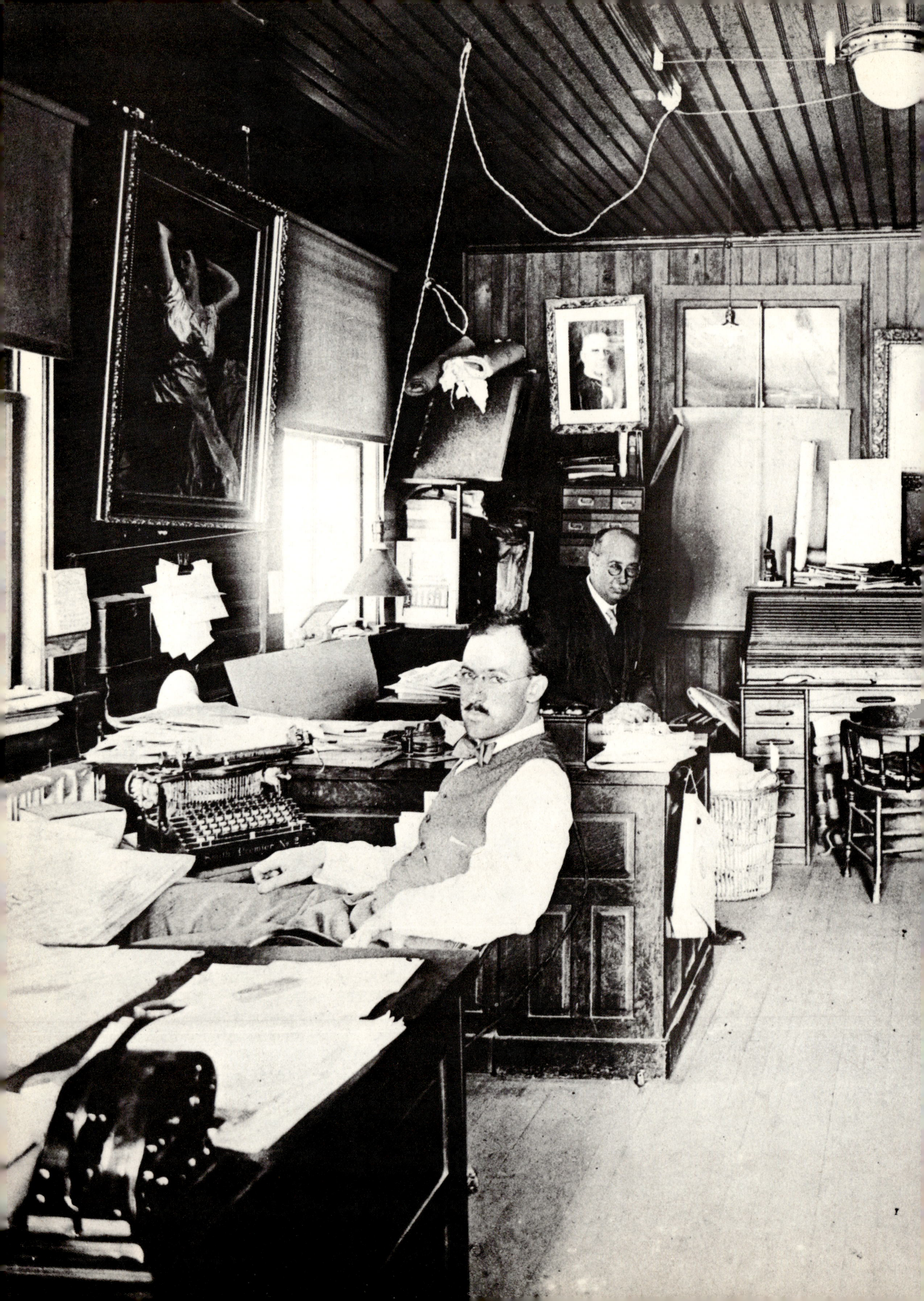

"The main thing is to have this paper represent the average thought of the best people of Emporia and Lyon County in all their varied interests," William Allen White announced in 1895 upon assuming the editorship of the Emporia, Kansas, *Gazette*. White's shrewdness, insight, and tart, wry humor—the storied virtues of the small-town newspaper editor— soon gained him a national following. A good editor who obeyed White's dictum made his office into Main Street's communications center. For four generations the Rotch family has performed that function in Milford, New Hampshire. At left is the cluttered office of the Milford *Cabinet* early in the century. At the typewriter is Arthur B. Rotch and beneath the President McKinley portrait is William Boylston Rotch, father and grandfather respectively of the present editor, William B. Rotch; the languid lady in the portrait is unidentified. The press room with its potbellied stove is visible through the doorway. Above are the quarters of the Port Jefferson, New York, *Echo*, at about the same date. By the hitching post is publisher A. Jay Tefft, with his entire staff at the right. The *Echo* faded away during the Great Depression but its handsome building survived and today houses a pharmacy.

WELLS FARGO BANK HISTORY ROOM

COLLECTION OF AL FRED DANIEL

At the center of much activity, and often enough right in the center of town, was the railroad depot. Below is the Jackson, Mississippi, station, photographed about 1914 by Albert Fred Daniel, who set up his panoramic camera next to the Illinois Central tracks as the crossing guard moved out to clear the way for an express. Daniel's tripod-mounted Cirkut camera was turned through an arc by a clockwork mechanism, the film being exposed as the mechanism wound it past a narrow slit. (Panoramic cameras such as this were favorites of small boys who, after the camera started its circuit for a group portrait, would duck out, race around to the far side of the group, and thus appear twice in the picture.) Another fixture in many small towns was a Wells Fargo express office, like the one at left in Columbia, California. This 1913 picture was probably taken by the express agent and features his family, an overloaded pigeonhole filing system, a useful horseshoe chart (by the stovepipe) from the Capewell Horse Nail Company of Hartford, Connecticut, and a door of puzzling proportions.

OVERLEAF: Instant subdivisions have a long history in California, as witness this example photographed at the turn of the century by an unknown hand. In the distance, beyond the roughed-out grid pattern and sprouting street signs, is Bakersfield, 1900 population 4,835 and obviously due for an upsurge.

COLLECTION OF DAVID R. PHILLIPS

KERN ST.

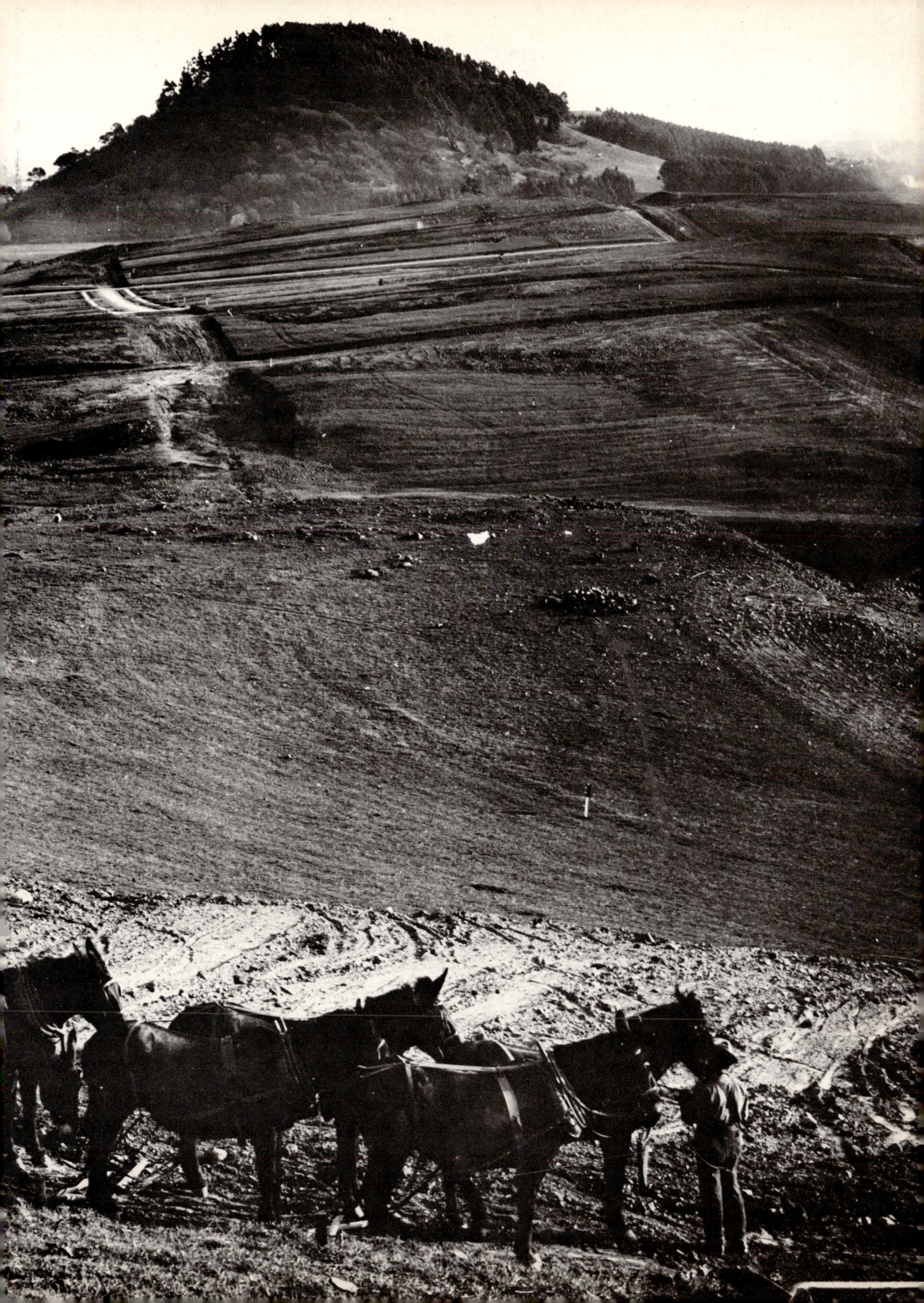

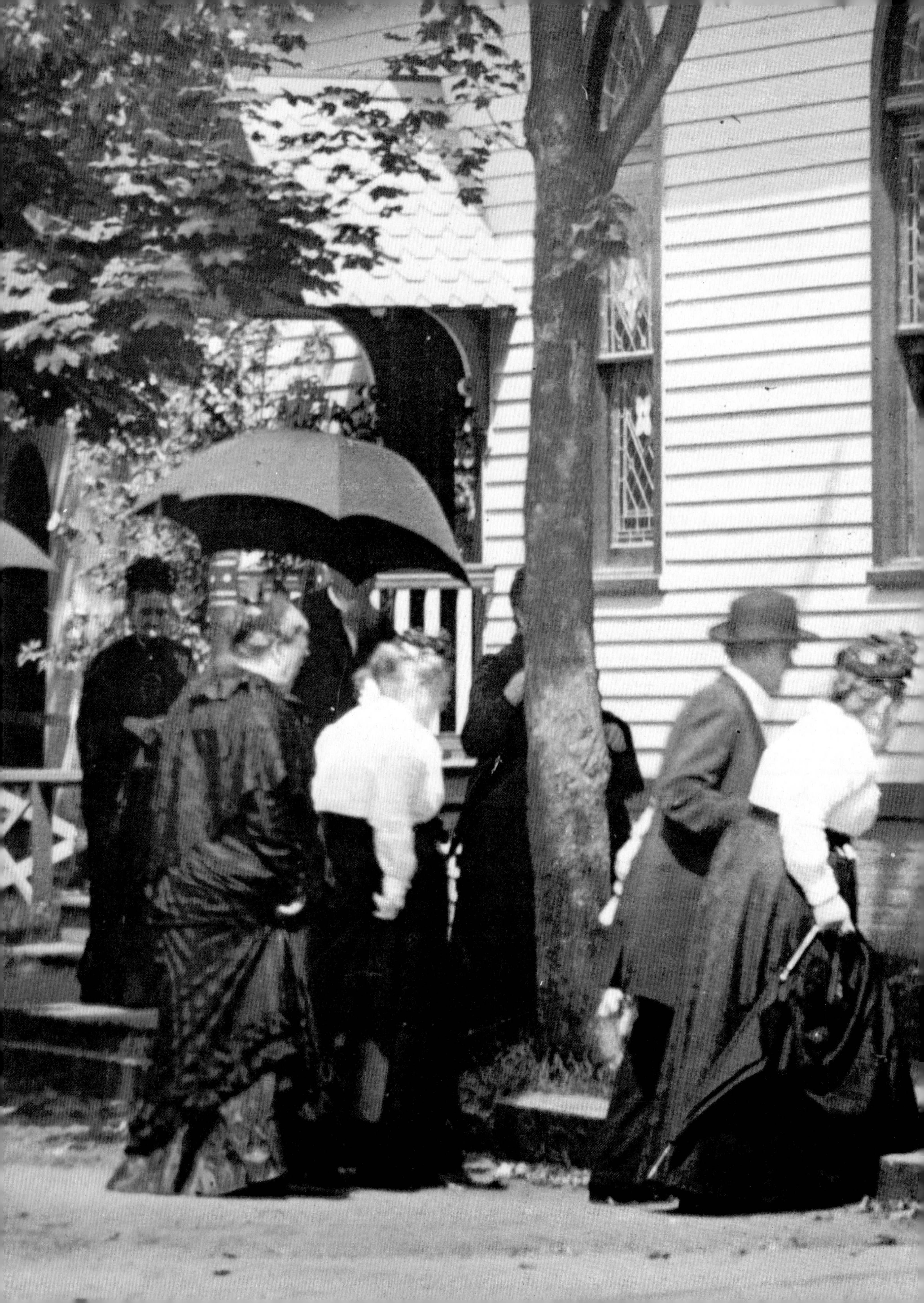

CHAPTER
2
All Around the Town

There was a comfortable, predictable rhythm to the pattern of daily life in a small town that bred confidence in the natural order of things. "Life seems to be sustained by rhythm, upset by its changes, weakened by its loss," Henry Seidel Canby observed, and in 1900, in small-town America, the rhythm was intact; by all reports, no one there was suffering from Future Shock. This chapter takes a look at that everyday routine.

One element of consistency in the pattern was church-going. Among Protestant faiths a standard Sabbath schedule included services both morning and evening as well as Sunday school for all. The Methodists pictured here in their summer finery are on the way to services in Ocean Grove, New Jersey, about the turn of the century. Most likely they would be returning at midweek for a prayer meeting. Theirs was a busy schedule, inspired not only by piety but by the major role of the church in community social life.

The greatest single influence on daily routine, however, was the cycle of the seasons. Replenishing fuel supplies, putting in the garden, filling the icehouse, and dozens of other chores had seasonal peaks and valleys. With central heating in its infancy and air conditioning yet to be conceived, seasonal extremes struck with their full force. Wintertime in the northerly latitudes required stubborn endurance and a strong survival instinct. In Cloquet, Minnesota, hometown of the writer Walter O'Meara, old-timers described the climate as "eight months of winter and four of poor sledding." Preparing for a northern Minnesota winter, recalls O'Meara, was like preparing for a siege: "Fall was a time of 'digging in,' of putting up storm doors and windows, cleaning flues and chimneys, stuffing the woodshed to its roof, laying in a supply of coal, and stocking the cellar with food enough to last until the return of spring." Equal forebearance was needed to survive an Iowa heat wave or August in Georgia. In such times, parasols and umbrellas were pressed into service as sun shields, and everyone who could "retired" to the deepest recesses of their shaded porches with palm fans and lemonade close at hand.

The seasonal rhythms also affected that majority of towns whose economic lifeblood was fortified by agriculture. The way Americans made their living was undergoing a major shift at the turn of the century. Between 1880 and 1910 the percentage of factory workers in the nation's total work force rose from under 22 per cent to more than 28 per cent and in trade and transportation from 11 to 20 per cent; in the same period, the percentage of agricultural workers among the gainfully employed declined from 44.4 to less than 33 per cent. This continuing upheaval in the work force would in time profoundly change small-town life, but for the moment its effects were masked by another fact: in absolute numbers the farming population was still growing. There were 12.5 million Americans who listed agriculture as their gainful occupation in 1910, an increase of more than 2 million over the previous census figure (the total rural population in 1910 was just under 50 million), and for those millions the nearest town remained marketplace and shipping center.

With his stock requiring daily care, a farmer's "range" was limited to the distance he could travel and return in a single day, and in the age of the horse this meant that whatever town was within a radius of a dozen miles or so was the town where he took his business. That business fluctuated seasonally. At harvest time farm wagons were lined up around the depot or the grain elevator or the cotton gin, and the better the crop the more the town prospered in its middleman's role. So impressive was the 1909 wool clip in the area around Roswell in New Mexico Territory, for example, that the town photographer was commissioned to memorialize it (page 70). Springtime brought with it a demand for seed and fertilizer and farming implements and mortgage money, and in the winter the harness maker, the blacksmith, and the carriage builder could expect extra business as farmers repaired, refurbished, and replaced equipment. The size of the crowd on the traditional farmers' Saturday in town—and thus the business volume of the Main Street merchants—also varied seasonally.

If the national shifting of employment patterns was a time bomb ticking away quietly in small-town America during the early years of the century, a second radical shift in the economic picture was already in evidence. Here again the root cause was industrialism, but the trigger was the railroad. The revolution that brought an end to the small town's long-standing and cherished self-sufficiency, replacing it with an economy that was interdependent, traveled by rail.

As major industries grew and established national marketing and advertising capabilities, their products were hauled by train from one end of the nation to the other. Towns that won the tooth-and-claw competitions for a rail connection in the hope of gaining jobs and population soon noted changes in their overall employment pattern. The kind of small industries that had traditionally made a town self-sustaining—tannery, packing house, distillery, furniture plant—discovered that they could not contend against the flow of those products arriving from faraway factories. Many local artisans, characterized by William Allen White as "little masters who made their own wares and peddled them to their neighbors," were also pushed out of business by the goods being unloaded down at the depot and had to shift to other lines of work. The shoemaker, unable to compete against the mass-produced oxfords and work boots flooding out of the factories of Lynn, became a shoe repairman; the tailor who hand-crafted Sunday suits for farmers and gentry alike became a retailer of ready-made clothes. Of course, not all the skilled artisans were overrun by the industrial revolution, and the following pages illustrate some who continued to flourish.

As real as these changes were, they came gradually and their effects did not cause sudden tidal waves in town economies. And in the event, the industrial miracle that was bringing forth bathtubs and indoor plumbing and electric lights and plush Grand Rapids parlor sofas was greeted with open arms. What did trouble many Main Street merchants, however, was that so much of the merchandise arriving at the depot was coming from one source—the mail-order house. Montgomery Ward, which pioneered the business in 1872 (Sears, Roebuck entered the field fourteen years later), took dead aim at farmers and small-towners, and the combination of low prices and wide choice was fierce competition indeed for local stores. In his *Main Street on the Middle Border*, Lewis Atherton has reconstructed the mood of these local retailers. "They were convinced that if mail-order houses continued to prosper," writes Atherton, "every country town would be reduced to a post office, blacksmith shop, doctor's office, and a grain elevator. Land values would decline and monopoly would rule the land. Only the railway depot would grow in size under the new regime."

In the Nineties, usually considered to be squarely in the middle of the Good Old Days, weightier developments than mail-order catalogs jarred the smooth rhythms of daily life in a great many towns. The decade began confidently enough. In the Plains states, wrote William Allen White in his *Autobiography*, "it seemed to the people in the towns, and to the better class of farmers . . . , that life would go on about as it was for those whom hard work, good luck, and God's mercy had assigned to places in the upper social stratifications of a classless democratic society." Then the storm broke. Heavy indebtedness and deflation drove countless farmers and small businessmen, especially in the West and the South, into desperate corners, and their sufferings were reflected in one country town after another in the form of bank failures, business foreclosures, and empty, weedy building lots. The financial panic of 1893 now crashed down upon the nation, pushing it into the worst depression of its young life. "Country towns had become charnel houses and the counties that surrounded them had become places of dry bones," concludes Michael Lesy in *Wisconsin Death Trip*. White was shocked by the look of things in Kansas. "The whole countryside was shabby, drab, and shopworn; the farmers were in revolt; the townspeople were bewildered and down at the heel," he remembered. "Change and decay were about me." Only in 1897, after much political upheaval, did the nation climb out of the depression and return to its prosperous habits.

The average small town entered the new century functioning at an economic pace more relaxed than in the average city. Town economies ranged from the relatively simple servicing of the rural countryside through a more complicated mix of small industries and retail and service establishments, to heavily industrialized towns like Massillon, Ohio (whose work force appears in several of the following pictures), where iron foundries, rolling mills, machine shops, and equipment plants supported a 1900 population of just under 12,000.

A shortage of comparative data limits any analysis of working conditions in American small towns; across the country, wages and hours varied wildly according to occupation and the size and location of the town. The ironworkers pictured on pages 68-69 were probably in line with the national averages for their trade: a 55- to 60-hour work week for an annual wage of around $500. The boys in the picture would have earned considerably less. At Angle's grocery in Mansfield, Ohio, the hours were 6 to 6 six days a week, plus two evenings, and the owner was on hand most of that time. In his best year, during the First World War, John Angle netted $5,000, but that was far above his average. In Kansas on the eve of the new century a journeyman printer earned $8 a week—and a pound of steak cost him 10 cents, a pound of bacon 9 cents, and a frying chicken 15 cents. With exceptions, most notably in the grimmer of the mining and industrial towns, the typical small-town worker generally encountered better conditions, less pressure, and less impersonality than his fellow worker in the city. But he got no wealthier.

Regardless of how they made their living, most people made it part of their daily routine to find time to see what was going on around town. No stop at the post office or the druggist's was complete without an exchange of views on the weather or the latest bit of local news. The fact that such establishments as the general store, the livery, and the barbershop accommodated without question visitors (invariably described as "loafers" by the better element) whose sole objective was gossip and in cold weather keeping warm at the potbellied stove, suggests something about the pace of small-town life.

One of the favorite gathering places was the depot, and seldom did a train make a scheduled stop without an audience. Novelist Conrad Richter, who grew up in Pine Grove, Pennsylvania, observed that the railroad provided small-towners with a sense of adventure, a glimpse of the outside world. From Pine Grove's depot, he wrote, "the rails ran without interruption to palm trees and deep snows, to mountains and deserts, to eastern and western seaboards, and out on docks where liners left for alien shores." But there was more to it than that. "There was always activity generated or its expectation. The constant sound of steel wheels was reassurance that all was well. The going and coming of trains were the hands of the town clock, and engine whistles, the striking of the hours." Here was one more of the comfortable rhythms in the pattern of daily life.

WHALING MUSEUM, NEW BEDFORD, MASS.

The rhythm of life three generations ago was far more affected by the rhythm of the seasons than it is today. In Daytona, Florida (right), the residents of Ridgewood Avenue passed the drowsy hot days on their deep porches under shade trees hung with Spanish moss. (Ridgewood Avenue is now four lanes, its old charm quite gone.) Life was faster-paced in wintertime New England. In the scene above, two cutters move briskly along County Street in New Bedford, Massachusetts, in the 1890's; the photographer is unknown. The Florida picture, dating from 1904, may be the work of the famous Western photographer William Henry Jackson, part-owner of the Detroit Publishing Company, a major commercial picture agency of the period.

DETROIT PUBLISHING COMPANY COLLECTION, LIBRARY OF CONGRESS

STATE HISTORICAL SOCIETY OF WISCONSIN

COLLECTION OF ROBERT L. WEICHERT

48

Coping with Northern winters required a certain ingenuity. Roads were often made passable for sleighs and cutters by heavy, oak-planked snow rollers. The 1893 photograph at right, with Mason's general store and the Unitarian church in the background, was taken in Dublin, New Hampshire, by Henry D. Allison. Larger towns such as Bennington, Vermont (left), found that trolleys made effective snowplows. This is East Main Street, with the imposing Opera House in the background, about 1900, photographed by Wills White. Another winter task was filling the icehouse. The ice-harvesting scene above was taken by Charles Van Schaick at Black River Falls, Wisconsin, in the 1890's. After marking, the cakes were sawed out by hand, hauled to the icehouse, and insulated with sawdust and hay for summer use. The bridge carried the Chicago, St. Paul, Minneapolis & Omaha across the Black River.

COLLECTION OF ELLIOTT S. ALLISON

In towns where local pride and boosterism were strong, perhaps galvanized by the local paper, things were always being improved upon or at least spruced up. The picture below was taken in 1906 in Brookville, Indiana, by an amateur photographer named Benjamin Franklin Winans. The lightning rod apparatus atop the Presbyterians' steeple is getting a fresh coat of gilt at the hands of G. Henri Bogart, town sign painter; just how Mr. Bogart bridged that ladder gap to get down again is unknown. The building still stands, but its handsome steeple is gone. It was a great day in Watertown, Wisconsin, when they finished paving Main Street (right). The job of laying in each brick by hand was supervised by the no-nonsense foreman in the foreground. The picture was taken about 1900 by Henry Bergman, who, like Winans, was an amateur photographer. Bergman's full-time job was clerking in a Watertown store.

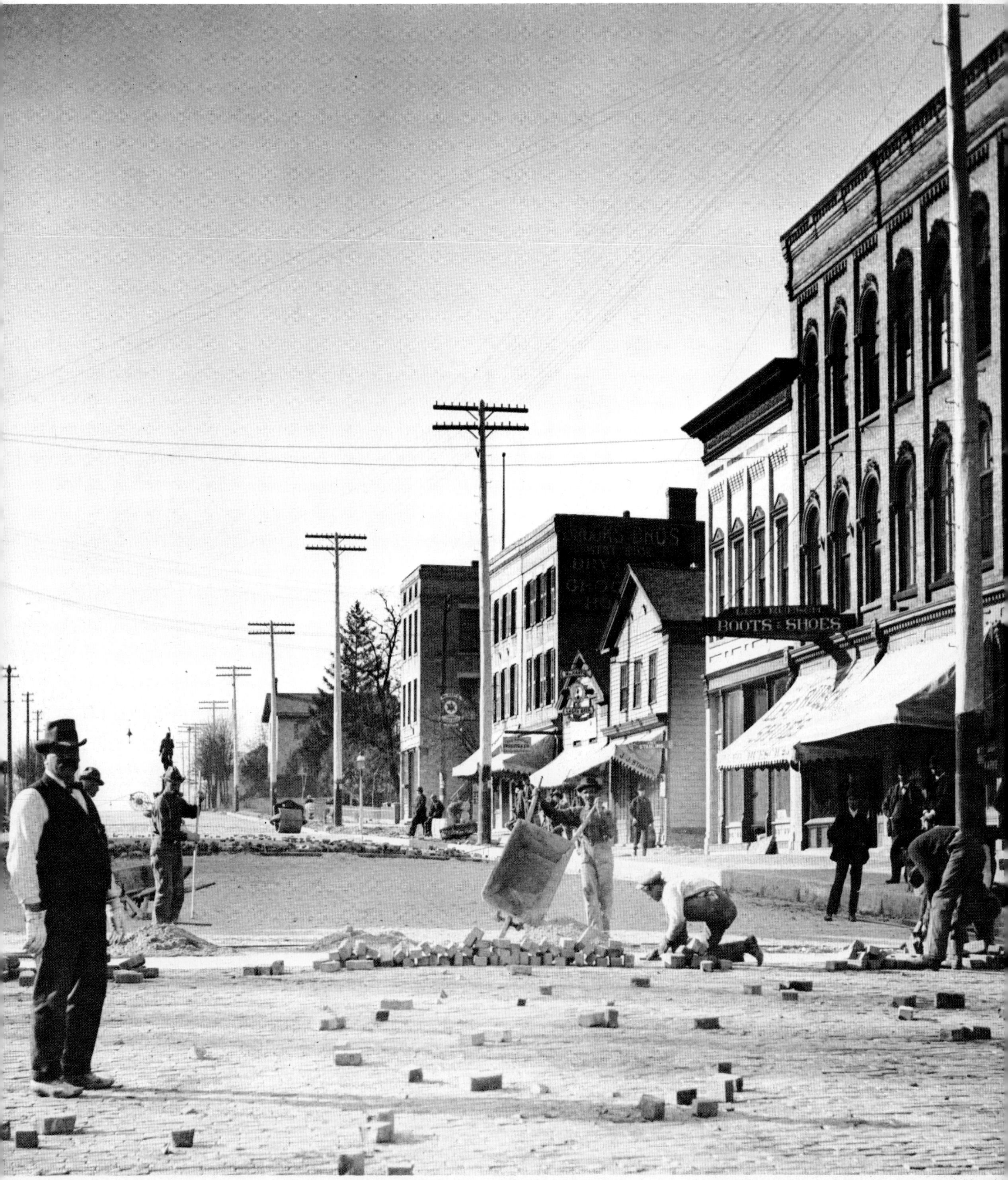
BOOTS & SHOES

Municipal services were limited, with priority to law and order and fire protection. Above is the county courthouse in Winchester, Kentucky; the watering trough is a reminder that this was bluegrass country. Below is the Massillon, Ohio, constabulary c. 1900, with the mayor (center) and his chief marshal in mufti. Opposite are the firemen of Mullan, Idaho, against a backdrop of the Bitterroot Range. Their carnations celebrate Decoration Day.

LIBRARY OF CONGRESS

53

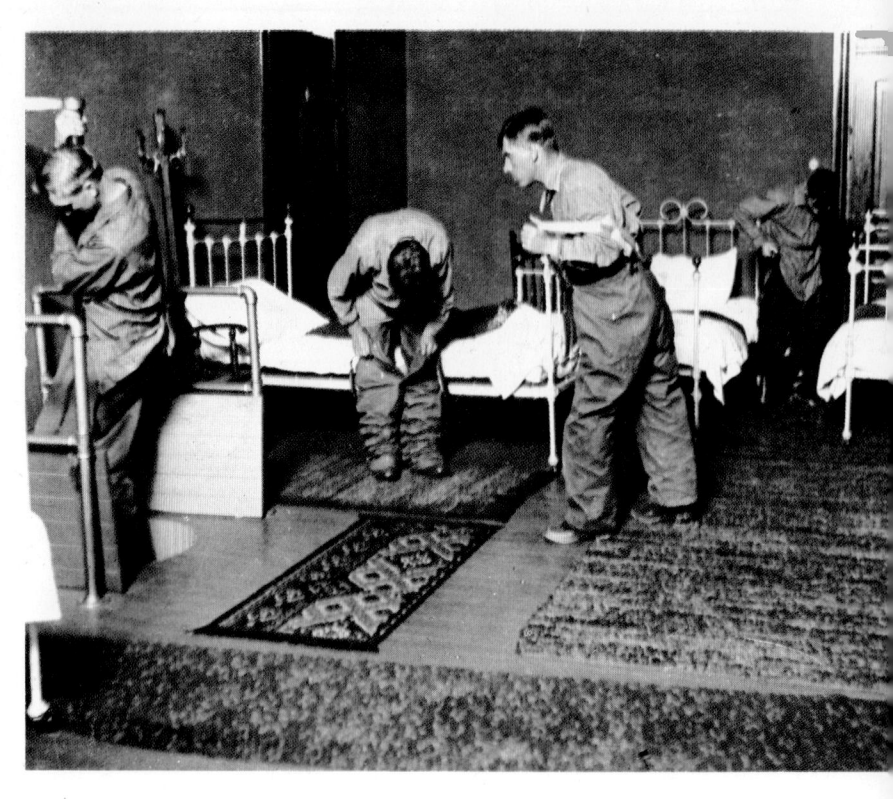

The Mullan fire department pictured on the previous page was a volunteer outfit, as were the departments in the vast majority of small towns. In growing communities with growing property values, however, the volunteers often gave way to paid professionals, who were better trained and more efficient. A place like Massillon, Ohio, for example, was becoming heavily industrialized and required efficient fire protection. The pictures above are from a series made about 1912 to demonstrate the Massillon department's professionalism. The substantial firehouse meals (left) were taken only a few steps from the apparatus. Then it was from the frying pan (on the floor) into the fire: the next scene is the dormitory seconds after the alarm sounded. Thanks to the famous brass sliding pole, the men were quickly at work harnessing their eager team to the hook and ladder. The fourth picture presents the safety-net crew in action, although it is assumed that in a real emergency the netmen would have spread out properly. At right is a firemen's convention in 1889, hosted by the Cumberland fire company of Carlisle, Pennsylvania. Among the polished apparatus parked along the main street are a hose carriage and a hook and ladder at the left, and, at the right, a second hose carriage and a splendid big Button & Blake steamer.

LIBRARY OF CONGRESS

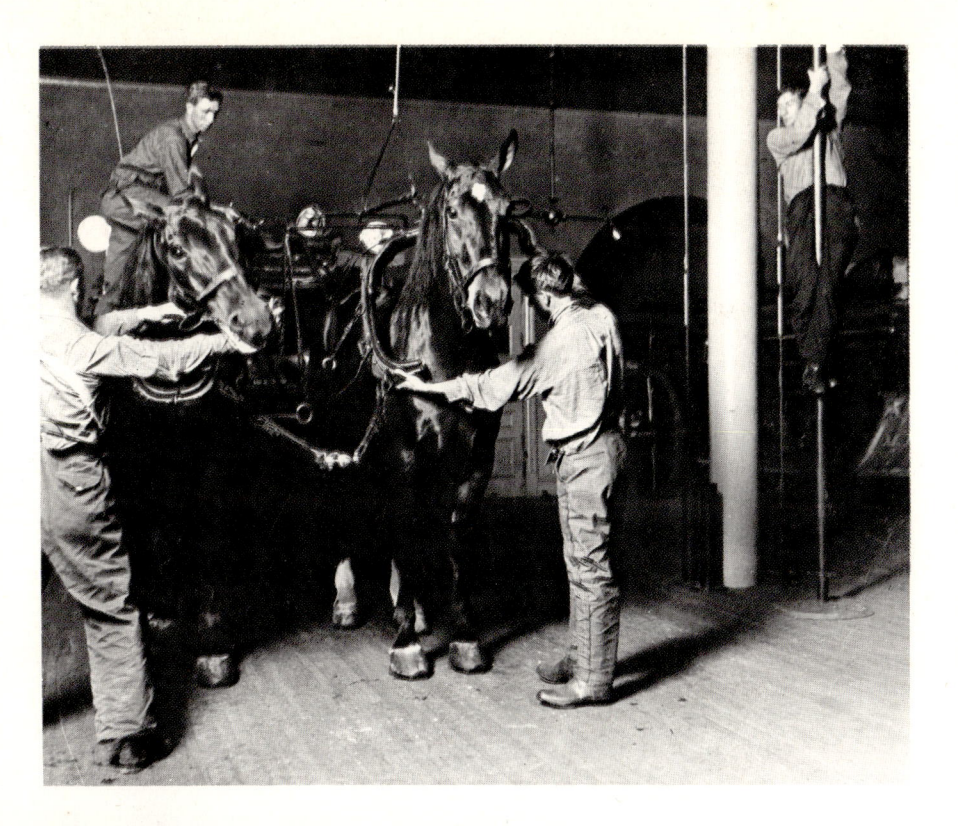

PHOTOGRAPHIC ARCHIVES, UNIVERSITY OF LOUISVILLE

COLLECTION OF EDITH LAFRANCIS

Once upon a time "we deliver" was the rule, not the exception. The Cliff Owen dairy farm (left), which served Winchester, Kentucky, was obviously a family operation, and it included a family of cats. The picture by A. J. Earp dates from about 1905, and it is likely that in those bottles was raw milk; the century was well along before pasteurization became universal. The coal deliverymen were photographed about 1909 by the brothers Alvah and George Howes of Ashfield, Massachusetts. A winter's supply of coal for an average house might run to two tons. The fine study of the village fish peddlar, date and place unknown, is by Nathan Lazarnick.

INTERNATIONAL MUSEUM OF PHOTOGRAPHY, GEORGE EASTMAN HOUSE

57

MASSILLON MUSEUM

MINNESOTA HISTORICAL SOCIETY

By 1900 the average American small town was well on the way to economic interdependency. Services, however, retained their individualistic touch. The lawyer in his courthouse office, the real estate agent upstairs over the bank, the doctor who routinely made house calls all remained part of the daily scene. No doubt these three professional men were also on a first-name basis with their fellow townspeople. The piano tuner, one Downing, had his portrait made in Theodore Teeple's Massillon, Ohio, studio. At center is a Stillwater, Minnesota, pharmacist, photographed in 1910 by John Runk. The tools of his trade bear direct, no-nonsense labels: Sedative No. 3, Bitter Tonic, Brown Mixture. Dentist Herbert Shafer posed for William L. Bennett in his office on the square in Navarre, Ohio, in 1899. Conveniently at hand are his pedal-operated drill and, affixed to the chair, the patient's spittoon.

COLLECTION OF DAVID R. PHILLIPS

DETROIT PUBLISHING COMPANY COLLECTION, LIBRARY OF CONGRESS

60

The range of trades undertaken by small-town artisans was remarkably varied. The scene at left was recorded in a Minnesota lumber mill by Silas Melander. Feeding the steam-driven saw was a high-skill, high-risk job. The net-menders were photographed in 1906 at Charlevoix, Michigan, a fishing port on Lakes Michigan and Charlevoix known for its spring smelt run. The skilled craftsmen below worked for the Beau Brothers carriage shop of Winchester, Kentucky.

OVERLEAF: In the pre-auto age, all the blacksmithing and stabling and the largest share of the transport equipment—wagons, carriages, harness, and the like—were supplied locally. The establishment of W. L. Lovejoy & Company of Milford, New Hampshire, painted, lettered, and customized vehicles from lowly bakery wagons to elegant coaches. The picture was taken *c.* 1910 by L. E. Lindsay and J.L.B. Smith, self-styled landscape photographers of nearby Nashua.

W. L. LOVEJOY & Co.
CARRIAGE TRIMMING AND HARNESS MAKING
BREAD. CAKES
CRACKERS

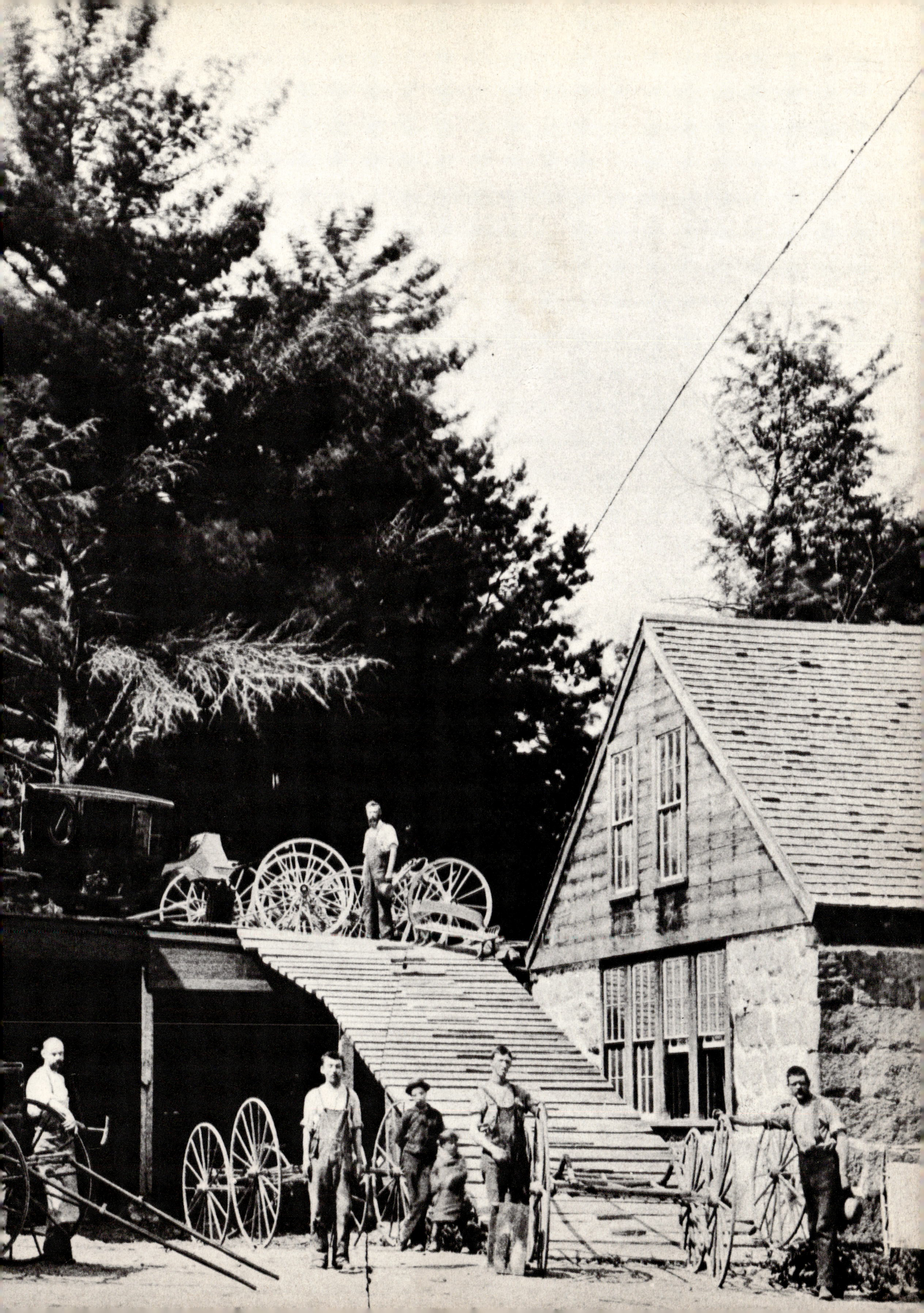

COLLECTION OF EDITH LAFRANCIS

STATE HISTORICAL SOCIETY OF WISCONSIN

The establishment of mills and factories, a development much desired and fervently pursued by growth-minded towns, was usually followed by the arrival of "outsiders" to supply the needed cheap labor—a development rather less desired by the local people. Soon there were enclaves, native-born as well as foreign-born, across the tracks or down in the hollow, often enough derisively labeled Hunkytown or Darktown or the like. The Irishwomen on the facing page operated a boardinghouse that fed workers in a Massachusetts mill village; the picture was made by the Howes brothers in 1895. The German seamstresses above were photographed in Watertown, Wisconsin, by Henry Bergman.

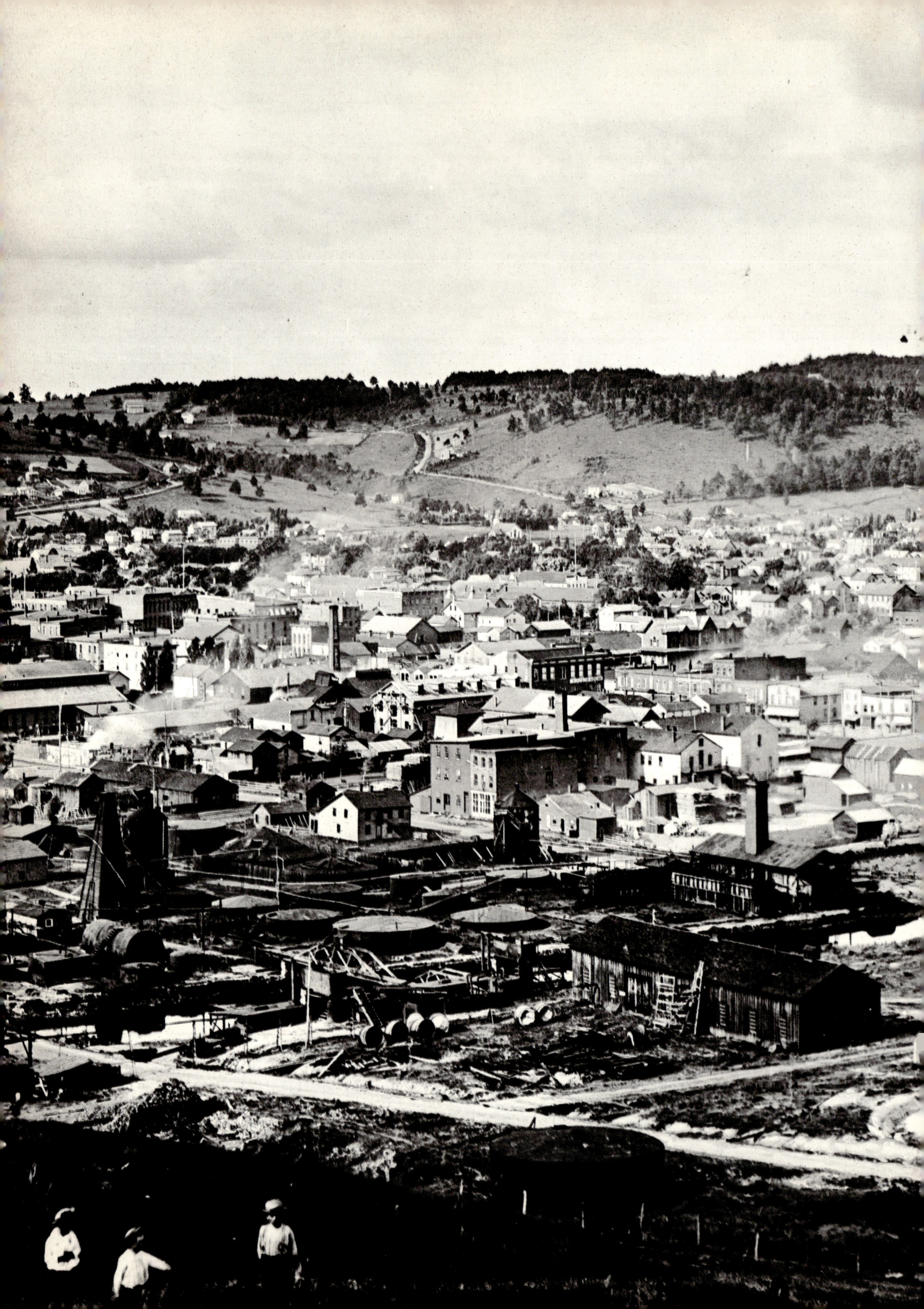

Many single-industry towns became that way for the very good reason that they were sited atop a rich natural resource. Here are two examples. Opposite is Titusville, Pennsylvania, which in 1859 was a village of a few hundred located two miles from the spot where Edwin L. Drake drilled his famous oil well. By the time John A. Mather took this panoramic view in the 1880's, it had outgrown its boomtown reputation as the "Sodden Gomorrah" to become the marketing, shipping, and refining capital of the Pennsylvania oil fields. The single major industry in Proctor, Vermont, was marble. Above is the orderly storage yard of the Vermont Marble Company, which employed nearly all the able-bodied workers among Proctor's 2,000-odd citizens when this stereo view was made in 1903.

OVERLEAF: This portrait of ironworkers at the Corns Rolling Mills in Massillon, Ohio, was taken not by the child-labor reformer Lewis Hine as might be expected, but by town photographer Theodore Teeple. It is one of a series he made of all the crews at the mill, commissioned by a proud company management. In 1910 almost 3,000 boys under sixteen held such jobs in the iron and steel industry.

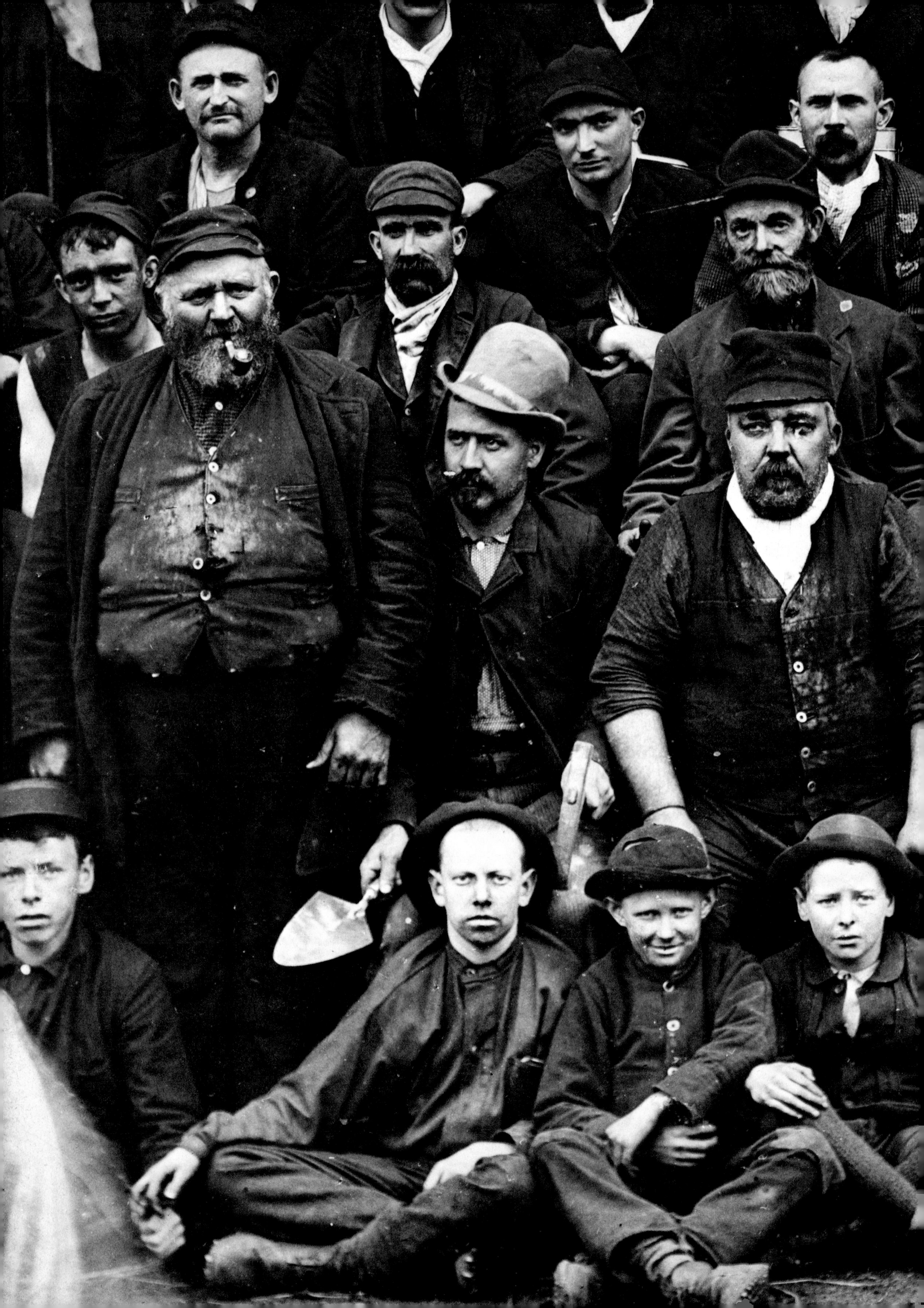

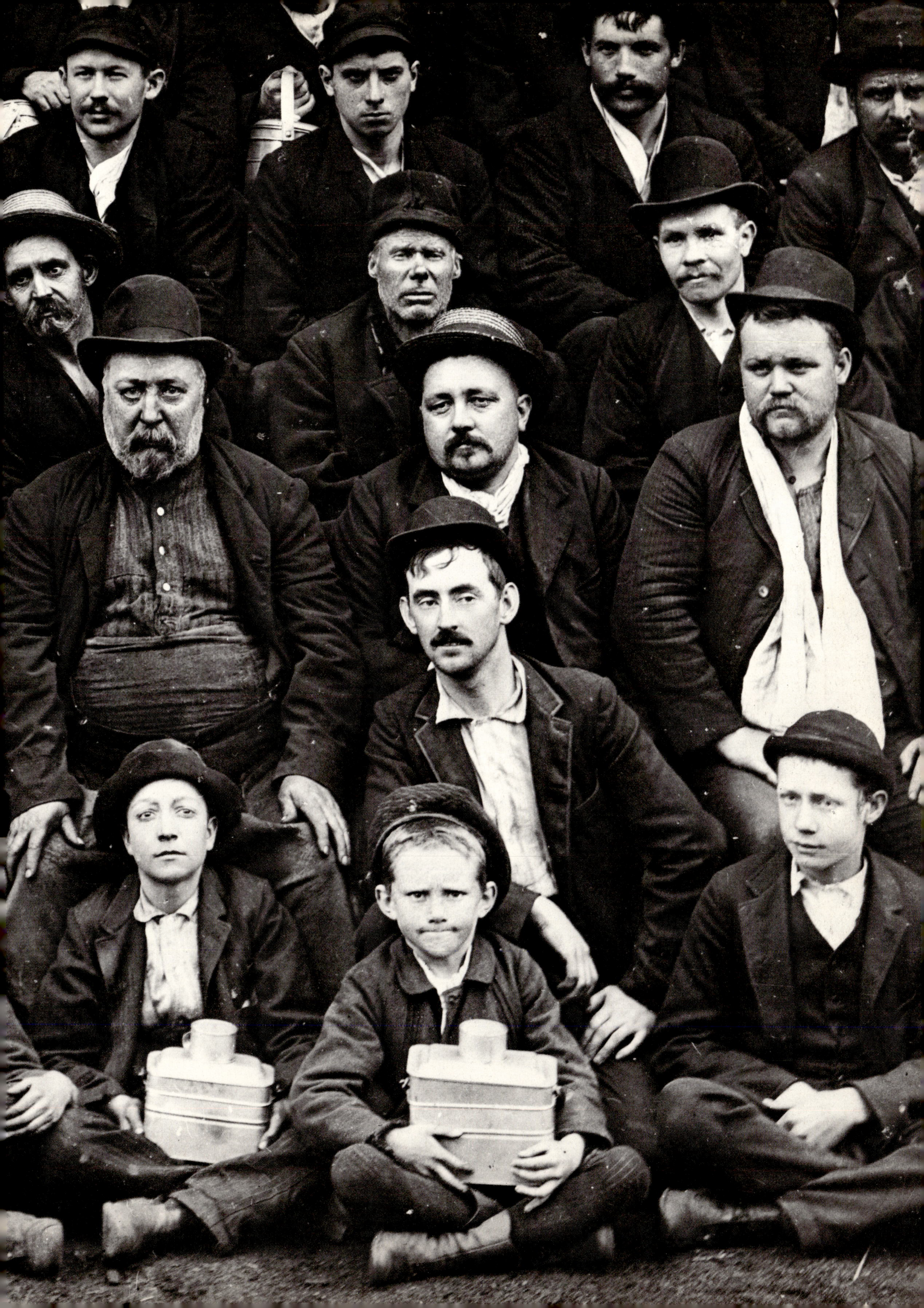

BROWN BROTHERS

There were industrial towns like Massillon and one-industry towns like Proctor scattered across America, but the primary economic function of the majority of small towns around the turn of the century was still serving as agricultural marketing centers. Roswell in New Mexico Territory (left) is an example. In 1909 E.H. Wilkinson set himself up across the street from the ornate façade of Roswell's Grand Central hotel to record the arrival of 85,000 pounds of wool for shipment east by rail. (The drummer's flivver at right in the picture is a Ford pre-Model T offering.) The hogs (top right) being driven to the butcher's were photographed by Charles Van Schaick in Black River Falls, Wisconsin. Putt Telfer took the picture of hay wagons (lower right) on Main Street in Cooperstown, New York, about 1910. The hay was on its way to the depot for dispatch to dairy farmers downstate and in New Jersey. Standing at center is a certain Mr. Marsh, who had nothing to do with buying or selling hay; he happened by just as Telfer deployed his camera.

OVERLEAF: The role of the town as a mecca for the surrounding countryside is perfectly captured in this scene. The farmers are gathered for a fair in March, 1908, in Princeton, Wisconsin.

STATE HISTORICAL SOCIETY OF WISCONSIN

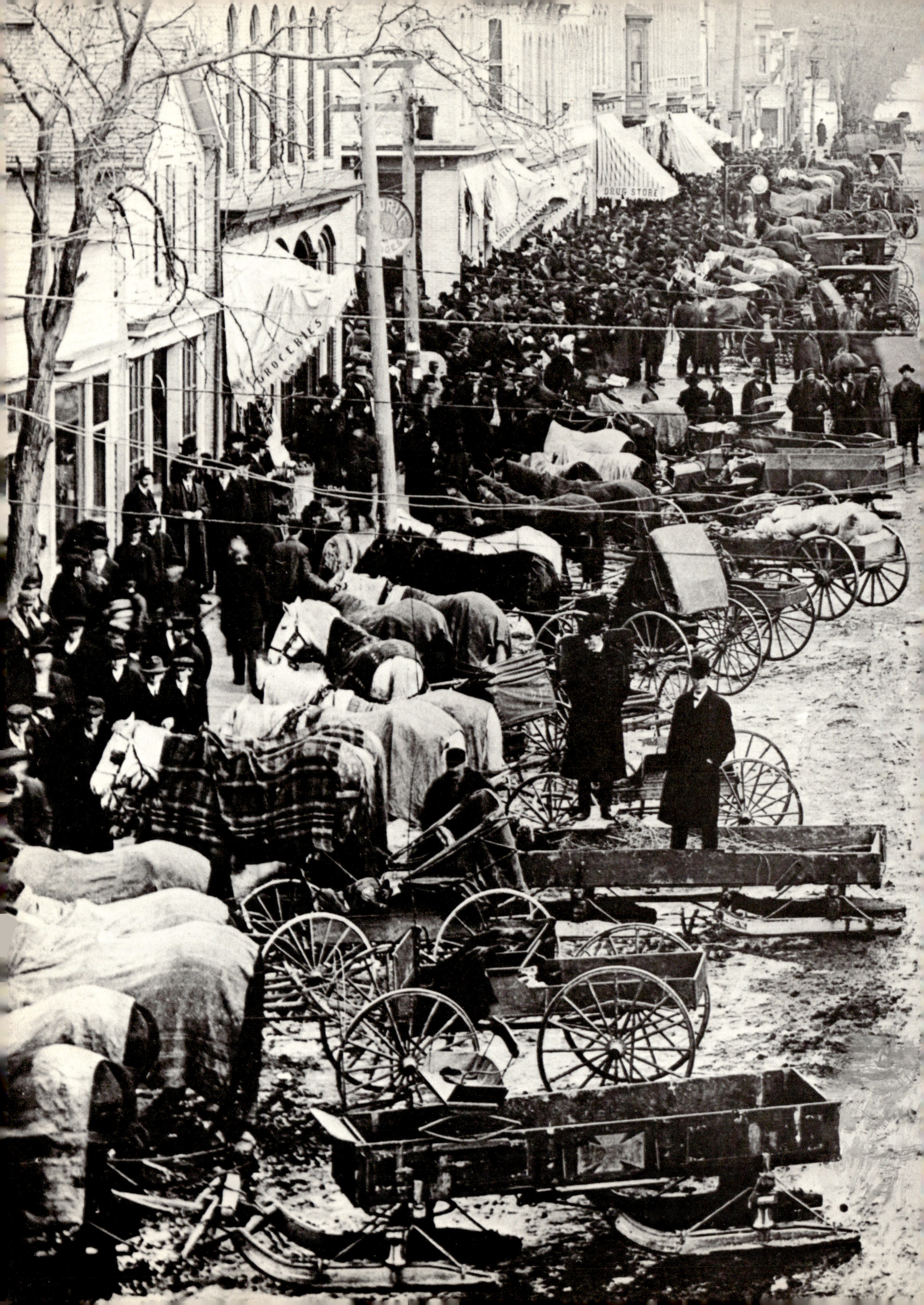
DRUG STORE
GROCERIES

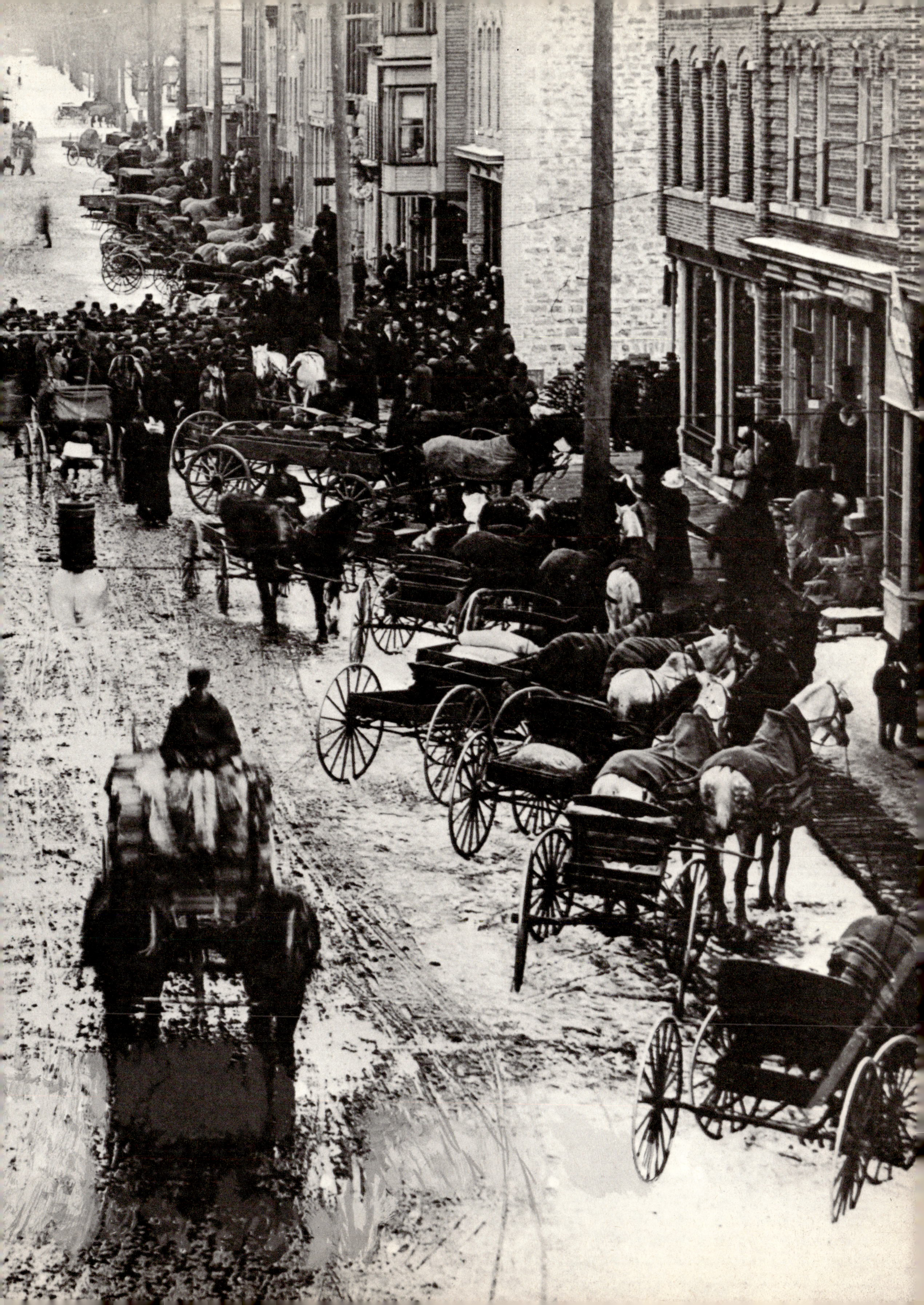

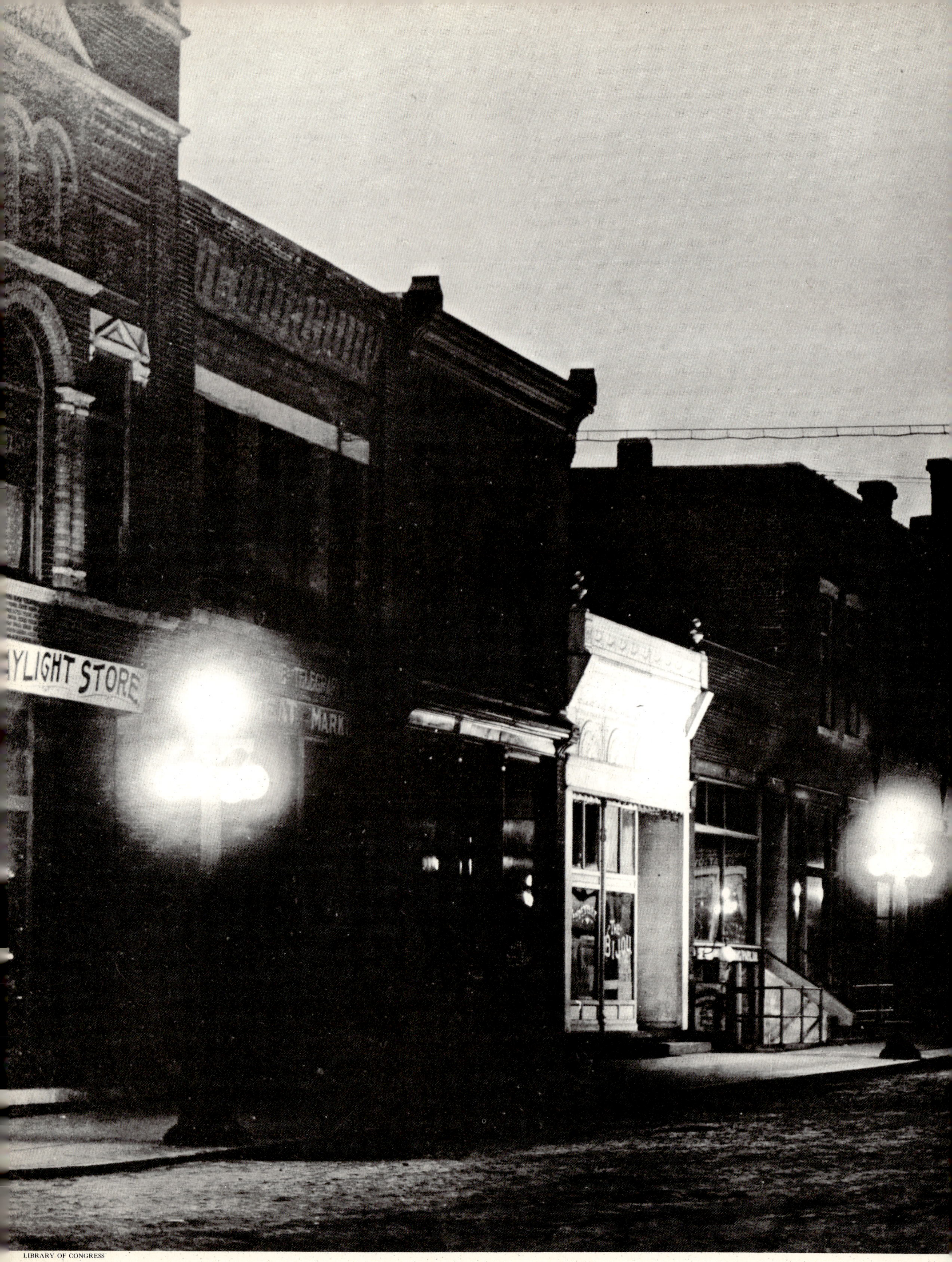

LIBRARY OF CONGRESS

In town as on the farm, it was early to bed, early to rise. The date is 1911, the place is Harlan, Iowa, at midnight, and the stage is deserted in the glare of the arc lights.

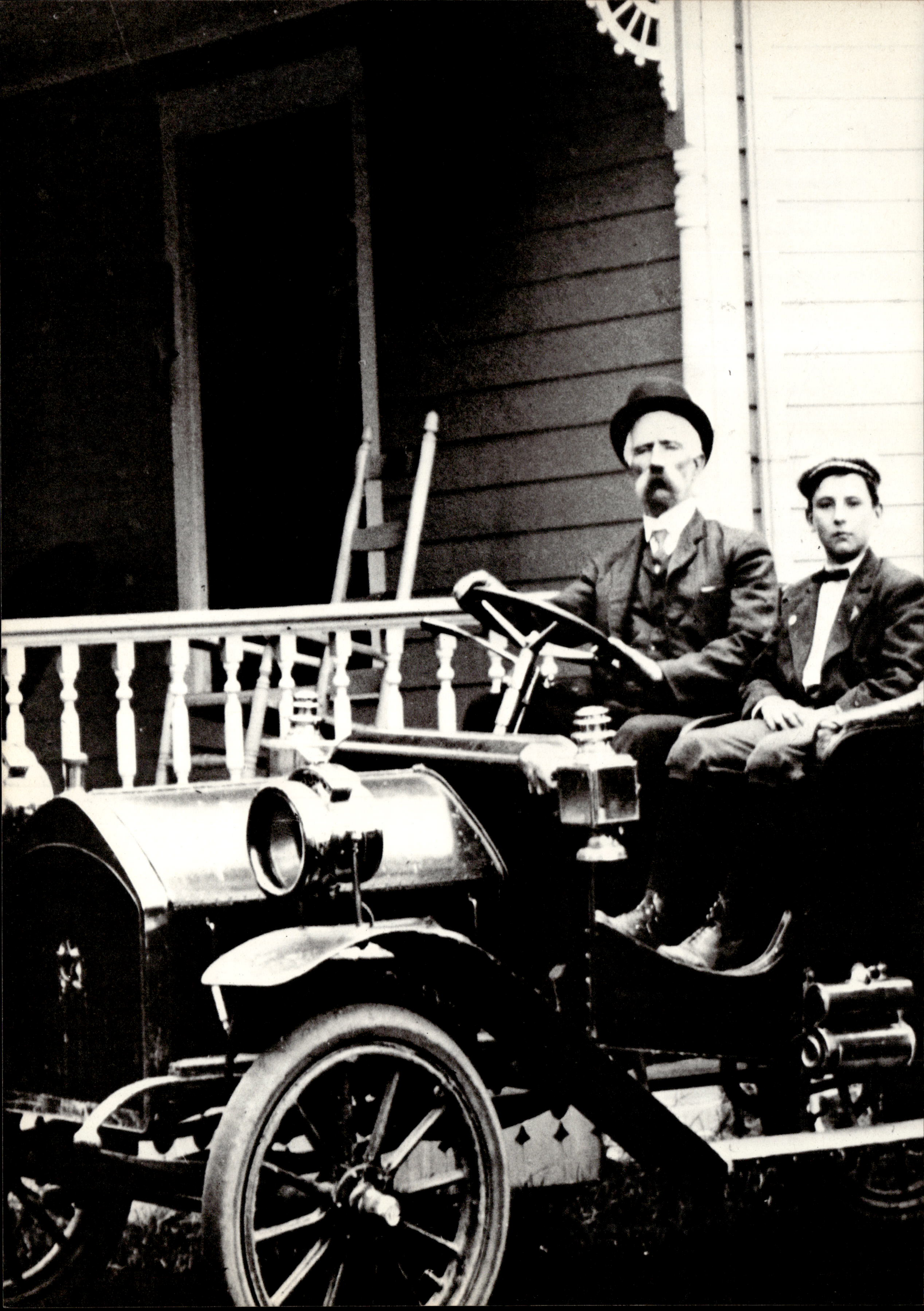

CHAPTER

3

Home and Family

Americans of an earlier day exhibited a deep, proud attachment to the homeplace and to family ties, and that most quoted of Edgar Guest's lines is an appropriate epigraph for the pages that follow. Once settled in, most families tended to stay settled, entirely willing to invest a heap o' livin' in a house t' make it home.

Here, looking calmly into Charles Van Schaick's camera, is the Eugene Greenlee family of Black River Falls, Wisconsin. The touring car is a Northern, 1906 or 1907 model, proclaimed "silent and dustless" by its Detroit manufacturer; from Mr. Greenlee's prideful pose behind the wheel, it may have been a new purchase ($1,800) and the reason for the picture. The Greenlee place was everything a house of the period should be: comfortably proportioned and discreetly gingerbreaded, with a rocking porch and an organdy-curtained parlor on the front and a working porch on the back. Whatever else might be said of the Greenlee family, Van Schaick's portrait suggests that for the time and place, it had gained its fair share of the world's goods.

The small-town photographer earned his bread and

butter recording the benchmarks of family life—birth, marriage, children, death. Human life remained a fragile stem as the twentieth century began. Infant mortality was running at the rate of 10 to 15 per cent during the century's first decade, and due in part to that fact, the life expectancy of a male born in 1900 was 46.3 years and of a female 48.3 years. Outbreaks of influenza and pneumonia carried off more than 153,000 Americans in 1900, nearly 12 per cent of the deaths from all causes that year, and tuberculosis killed nearly as many. Thus it is not surprising that photographic likenesses of loved ones were cherished. Too often parents survived their child, and pictures like that on page 91 were the result; the framed photograph and the entry on the flyleaf of the family Bible comprised the visual remembrance of a brief life.

A number of the pictures that follow are the work of professional photographers such as Van Schaick, but there is also a scattering by talented amateurs who present an informal, candid view of family life in the Good Old Days. The wedding couple from Boonville, Missouri, posing with their gifts (pages 98–99), for example, was taken by the town doctor, Charles Swap, who seems to have been one of the early photography hobbyists. The pictures by Mrs. Jeanette Bernard, mentioned in the introduction, first appear in this chapter. Isabel Walker Drake was still another devoted amateur, whose charming record of one family's life about the turn of the century was preserved in the picture albums of her three daughters. The Drake family lived in Corning, New York, and maintained a rambling summer "compound" on Keuka Lake in the Finger Lakes region. Theirs was certainly a comfortable enough life (James A. Drake was a Corning banker), and Mrs. Drake's pictures suggest that it was a happy one as well.

The typical family home of the period was a two-story frame structure of six or eight rooms. "Such a house was not cluttered by machinery of any kind," explains the newspaperman R.L. Duffus in *Williamstown Branch*, his memoir of growing up in Vermont. "It was heated, if this word is correct, by a series of coal stoves; it was lighted by kerosene lamps; all its drinking water had to be brought from outdoors . . . ; its privy was reached by walking out through the woodshed, which was much better than wading through snow or dashing through the rain to the older-fashioned, really outdoors variety; its bathing facilities were a wash-tub luxuriously placed, in winter, in front of the kitchen stove." The back yard might encompass, in addition to woodshed and backhouse, a barn or storage shed, a chicken coop, a grape arbor, and a vegetable garden. Shade trees were much prized, and the lady of the house carefully tended the borders of petunias and pansies. There was invariably a front porch, furnished with rockers and gliders and perhaps encased in ivy or woodbine. Or more than one porch: his father's pride and joy, reports William Allen White, was the "hundred forty-four running feet of porches" that nearly encircled their house in Eldorado, Kansas. A front porch rocker offered the perfect vantage point to watch the world go by.

In *We Made It Through the Winter*, Walter O'Meara conducts a guided tour of the house in Cloquet, Minnesota, where he grew up early in the century. In the front hall, he relates, was a steer-horn hatrack (a gift from Uncle Will out West) and an umbrella stand decorated with varnished-over cigar labels. A stairway led to the three austerely equipped bedrooms on the second floor. Opening off the front hall was the living room, which doubled as a dining room when there was company, dominated by a large table that "served as a center at which we all gathered to play games, do homework, write letters, cut material for dresses, wrap Christmas presents, and so on." The most impressive feature of the living room, perhaps of the whole house, was its Radiant Home Base Burner, tall and imposing, with isinglass windows and intricately scrolled trim in gleaming nickel.

Adjoining the living room was his parents' bedroom and the seldom-visited parlor. "You entered our parlor," writes O'Meara, "by way of a wide archway curtained with strings of eucalyptus seeds and glass beads. This curtain was brought back from California by my Aunt Vic, and it will give you an idea of what our parlor was like." The furniture was heavy golden oak, and there was an upright piano and in the corner a glass-front bookcase. An ingrain carpet, "gay with cabbage roses," covered the floor. Scattered about was a miscellany of *objets d'art*, including a pink conch shell and a painted plaster bust of an Indian maiden. There was a stereoscope on the marble-topped table, and on the walls hung several oil paintings of sunsets or flowers, the work of the artistic Aunt Vic. "It is true that our parlor was excessively formal," O'Meara admits. "Yet I cannot say that I remember it without respect. It was, after all, where my mother entertained company; where my sisters had their birthday parties, with chocolate in tiny Haviland cups taken from the locked china closet only on very special occasions; where our Christmas tree stood, casting a wavering light over the room; and where my mother, at last, lay in her coffin."

If the typical front parlor was, as Russell Lynes concludes, "a family chapel for the sanctification of the household lares and penates," the kitchen was the acknowledged center of the familial routine. Most meals, except Sunday dinner and those occasions when there was company, were taken there, with everyone crowding around the big oilcloth-covered table. To the young occupants of those unheated upstairs bedrooms, there was no haven so welcome as a warm, richly aromatic kitchen on an icy school morning in January.

It was not unusual for the kitchen furnishings to include a rocker or a sofa, but it was the range that held center stage. Usually wood-burning but equally at home with coal, coke, or even corncobs, the kitchen range was a versatile performer. It kept the room cozily warm in winter—and blistering hot in summer. There was an oven and a broiler; six lids set into the polished top; a porcelain or copper-lined reservoir to heat water for various purposes, including Saturday's baths and Father's shaves; a "warming closet" flanking the stovepipe to keep food hot until served and to dry mittens; and assorted warming shelves and pot brackets—all of this sheathed in black iron and highly ornate nickel trim. In 1908, the prices for Sears, Roebuck's best-quality line of "six-hole full nickeled ranges" started at $29.87.

The home was the woman's domain, a fact of life as incontrovertible as the man's position as the family breadwinner. The job consumed nearly all her waking hours, and in that day of few laborsaving devices it was a trying physical challenge. "Here lies a poor woman, who always was tired; She lived in a house where help was not hired," runs an old piece of doggerel.

Her weekly schedule was traditional but not always religiously observed. Monday was wash day and Tuesday ironing day. The collected sewing and mending was Wednesday's task. Thursday was supposed to be reserved for the turn-of-the-century equivalent of doing one's own thing—embroidering, reading, resting. Friday was cleaning day and Saturday was devoted to baking. Sunday's major effort went into the preparation of the week's special meal. All these tasks, of course, were in addition to the day-in and day-out routine of meal preparation, general care of the family, and community activity. What was expected of a wife by family and community has been summarized by historian Lewis Atherton. "As an angel of mercy to neighbors in distress and an avenging instrument of gossip," he writes, "she maintained her family's influence in society and church affairs. She was economical of her husband's worldly goods, condemned the vanities of rouge and the sin of cigarettes, and got her washing on the line at an early hour on Monday morning. Most of all, she sought 'advantages' for her children, and operated as a matchmaker in behalf of her marriageable daughters. . . ."

In the era before convenience and processed foods, everything was prepared from scratch. Coffee was ground in the kitchen or in the grocery at the time of purchase. A random sampling of the many homemade items found in the larder might include noodles, pot cheese, elderberry wine, oatmeal, and root beer. In the cellar there was more provender—most of it out of the back-yard garden—"put up" for the winter: Mason jars and jelly glasses filling shelf upon shelf, and bushels of apples and cabbages and bins full of root vegetables. A full cellar was comforting security against outrageous fortune.

In small-town America, family ties were ties that bound. Especially in the older communities east of the Mississippi, several generations might be found close to the homeplace, if not under the same roof; nearly every family had a relative or two occupying the spare room. Reunions were major events on the calendar, and well attended. The closeness of the family circle was in part a consequence of the full-time struggle required to get by and to make do. Every family member shared in that struggle, and they worked, played, and prayed together.

No family day, not even reunion day, was more important than Christmas. It was customarily celebrated at the home of the family patriarch. In the case of Iowa poet Paul Engle, that meant at the family farm ten miles outside town, but whether on a farm or in town, the traditions were much the same.

The byword for the Engles' Christmas was *homemade*. The fresh-cut tree was trimmed with paper chains and apples and popcorn strings, and the gifts, according to Engle, "tended to be hand-knit socks, or wool ties, or fancy crocheted 'yokes' for nightgowns, . . . and there would usually be a cornhusk doll, perhaps with a prune or walnut for a face, and a gay dress of an old corset-cover scrap with its ribbons still bright."

And then there was Christmas dinner. "There are no dinners like that any more," Engle insists. "To eat in the same room where food is cooked—that is the way to thank the Lord for His abundance. . . . The air was heavy with odors not only of food on plates but of the act of cooking itself, along with the metallic smell of heated iron from the hard-working Smoke Eater, and the whole stove offered us its yet uneaten prospects of more goose and untouched pies. . . ."

Afterward mothers and aunts and the older sisters and nieces pitched in to clean up the kitchen, while the men lit up cigars and talked politics and the children went outside for sledding. Finally it was dusk and time for thank-yous and good-byes. It had been like every other Christmas—a day to remember and to cherish.

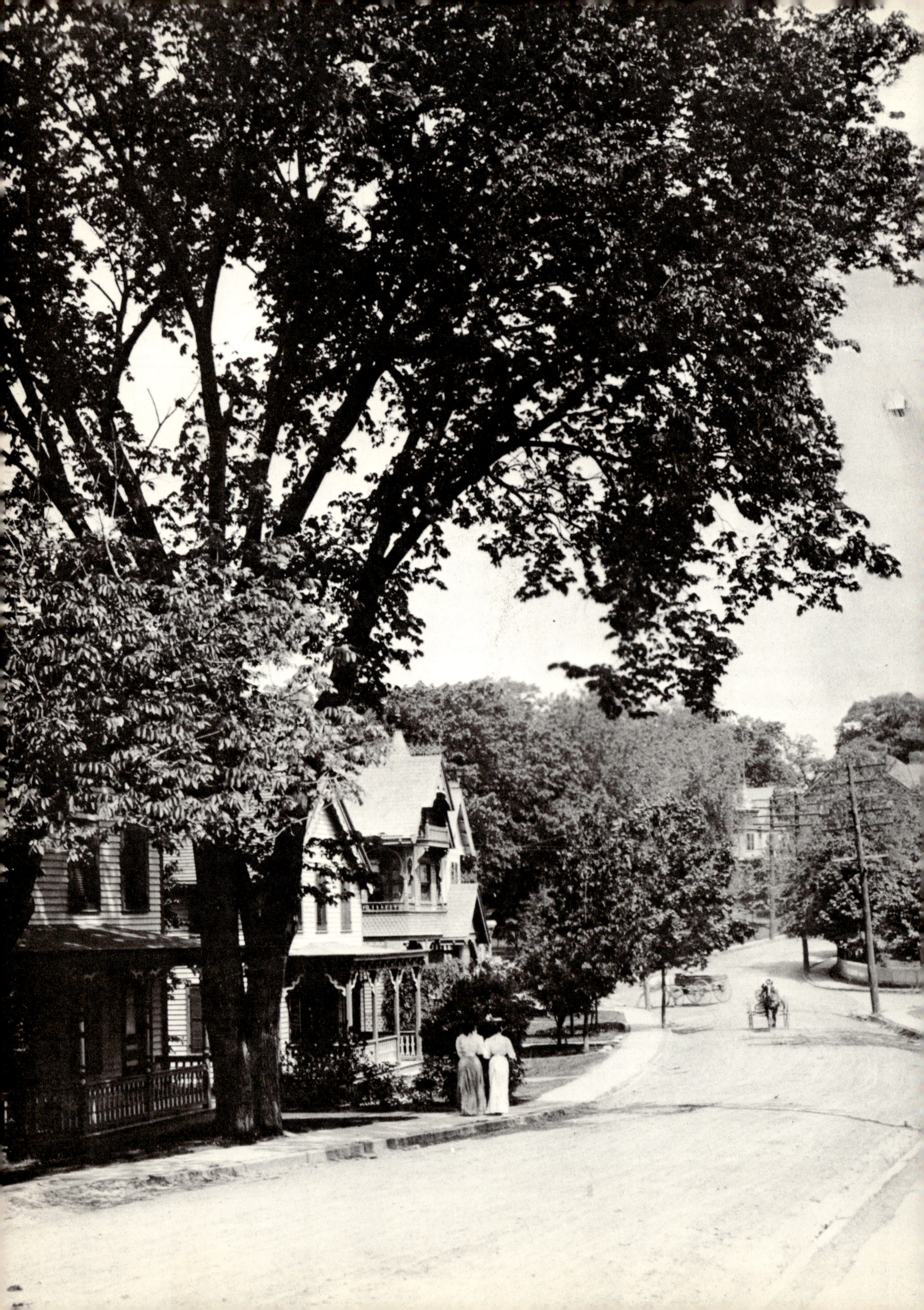

"Living on the wrong side of the tracks," like all clichés, is a phrase with a solid basis in fact. In many a town the poor were relegated by economic pressures to the least desirable land along the railroad, and by code and custom this was the neighborhood of portions of the population that, racially and ethnically, the majority considered undesirable. The black neighborhood below is literally by the side of the tracks, and there is no doubt it was the wrong side. This is Florida in the Nineties, taken by a photographer named George Barker. The small-town "nice" neighborhood was just as much a cliché, and a classic example is depicted at left. This is North Avenue in Fishkill on the Hudson, New York, in 1907. It is almost possible to hear the clip-clop of the horses and the buzzing of the honeybees in the wisteria.

The June and January photographs below were taken for a New England family named Wiley. Cutter, buggy, and old Dobbin were all kept in the attached barn. The woman dressed warmly for a winter's drive carries what appears to be a doctor's bag, and in the lower picture she sits in the shadowed interior of what was often called a doctor's buggy. Is this Dr. Wiley? There is no doubt that at the right is the Milton Wilson family of Massillon, Ohio. Mr. Wilson (he and his wife are visible amidst the luxuriant foliage) commissioned Theodore Teeple to make this family portrait about 1890, and the house steals the scene. Its abundant trim reflects the enthusiasm with which architects embraced the new woodworking machinery coming into use. A later owner converted the Wilson house to commercial purposes and installed a new façade, but the building survives today as the Massillon Museum's educational center.

Hartford Public Library.
Croton, Ohio

CANTERBURY, N.H., HISTORICAL SOCIETY

As a rule, when the members of a family were not out working or at school or doing essential chores they took their relaxation at home. Making music in the parlor are two New England ladies named Louise Lewton (playing the violin) and her daughter, Jessamine. Their glass-plate portrait was made about 1900 by Luther Cody, who turned a hobby into an occupation by becoming town photographer in Canterbury, New Hampshire. The family group at right found the back yard an ideal place to relax with needlework or a book. The picture is the work of the Howes brothers, who made the Connecticut Valley their beat. Below is Isabel Walker Drake's study of her daughter, her niece, and Dewey the dog enjoying the pleasures of a splendid front-porch swing. The scene is New York's Keuka Lake about 1908.

NEW HAVEN COLONY HISTORICAL SOCIETY

AMERICAN HERITAGE COLLECTION

At the turn of the century the position of the noble dog as man's best friend was secure—"The one absolutely unselfish friend that man can have in this selfish world," Missouri's Senator George Vest had announced in 1884. Here are three happy pairings. We know nothing of the Connecticut gentleman in the runabout above beyond the fact that he kept a smart rig. At left, a dog probably named Spot performs for his master, one of aviation pioneer Glenn Curtiss' entourage at Hammondsport, New York. The picture dates from about 1912. On the facing page is R.M. Miller and canine friend, of Apollo, Pennsylvania. Mr. Miller outdid himself with the decorations: not only was it the Glorious Fourth, but the town's centennial (1816-1916) as well.

COLLECTION OF MELVIN ADELGLASS

MASSILLON MUSEUM

Belle Johnson—or Miss Belle, as she was known to everyone in town—opened a photography studio in Monroe City, Missouri, in 1890 and for the next 55 years, until her death, she recorded what went on: weddings, christenings, funerals, young men marching off to World War I, then World War II. In her spare time Miss Belle dabbled in character studies, and the charming portrait above of three local women was one of the results. Every town had a compliment of old-timers who lived with family or went their independent way. Opposite is Philo Beecher of Seymour, Connecticut, long a local horse trader and now selling melons from his garden. Amateur photographer William C. Bryant took his portrait in 1895.

NEW HAVEN COLONY HISTORICAL SOCIETY

COLLECTION OF DAVID R. PHILLIPS

It was the common practice for a family to call in the photographer to formally commemorate the ceremonies of life and death. The baptism above took place in the Fox River at Elgin, Illinois, about 1900. The child's coffin opposite was carefully positioned for photographer Maude F. Martin against a backdrop of grieving family and friends. The scene is Lancaster, Wisconsin, c. 1912.

OVERLEAF: A photograph such as this would likely have been framed with a black "mourning mat" and added to the family mementos in the parlor. The mourners in this staged but nevertheless affecting tableaux are unidentified. It was taken at Rifle, Colorado, by Fred or Ola Garrison, an itinerant husband-and-wife photography team that covered the western part of the state early in the century.

STATE HISTORICAL SOCIETY OF COLORADO

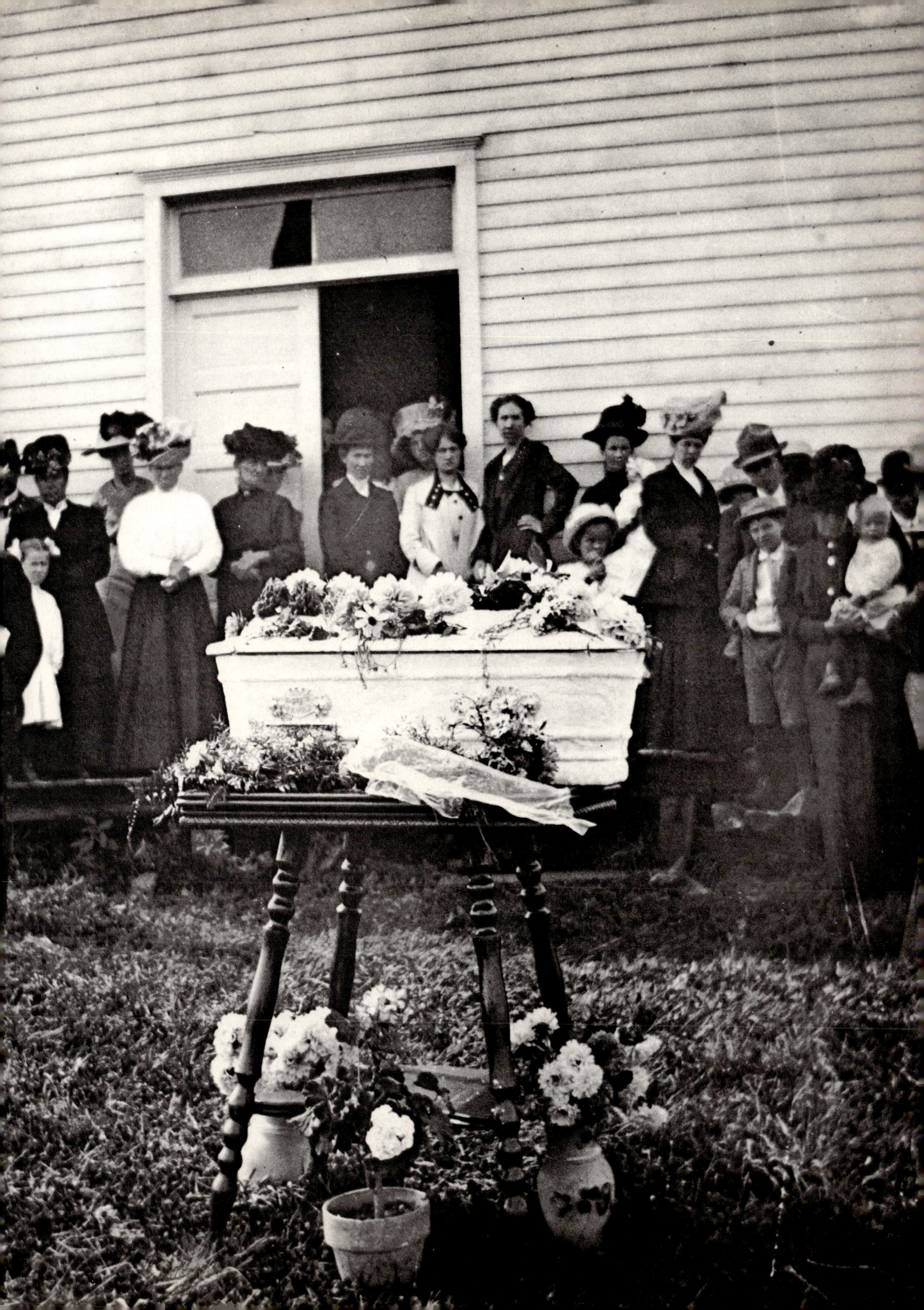

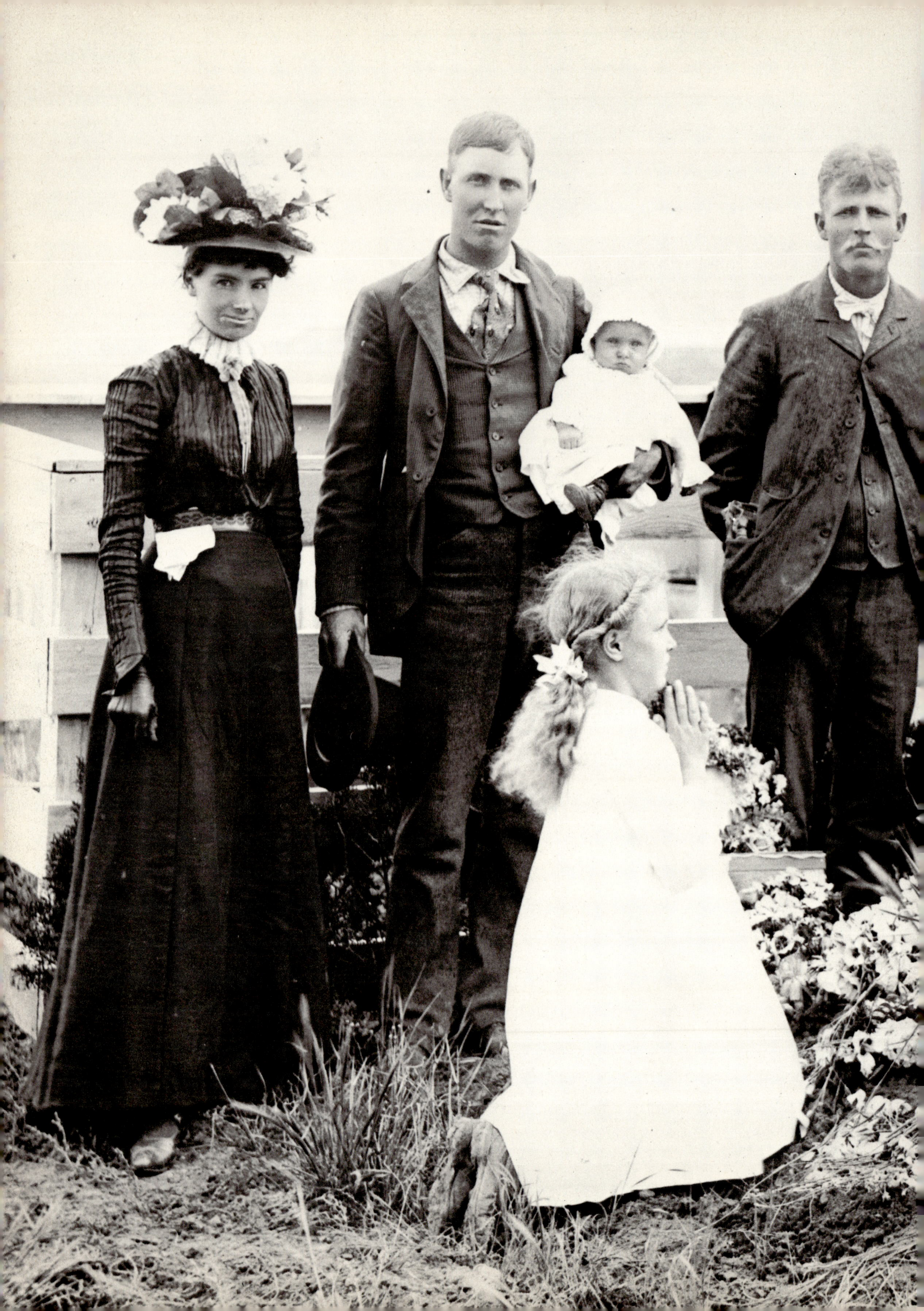

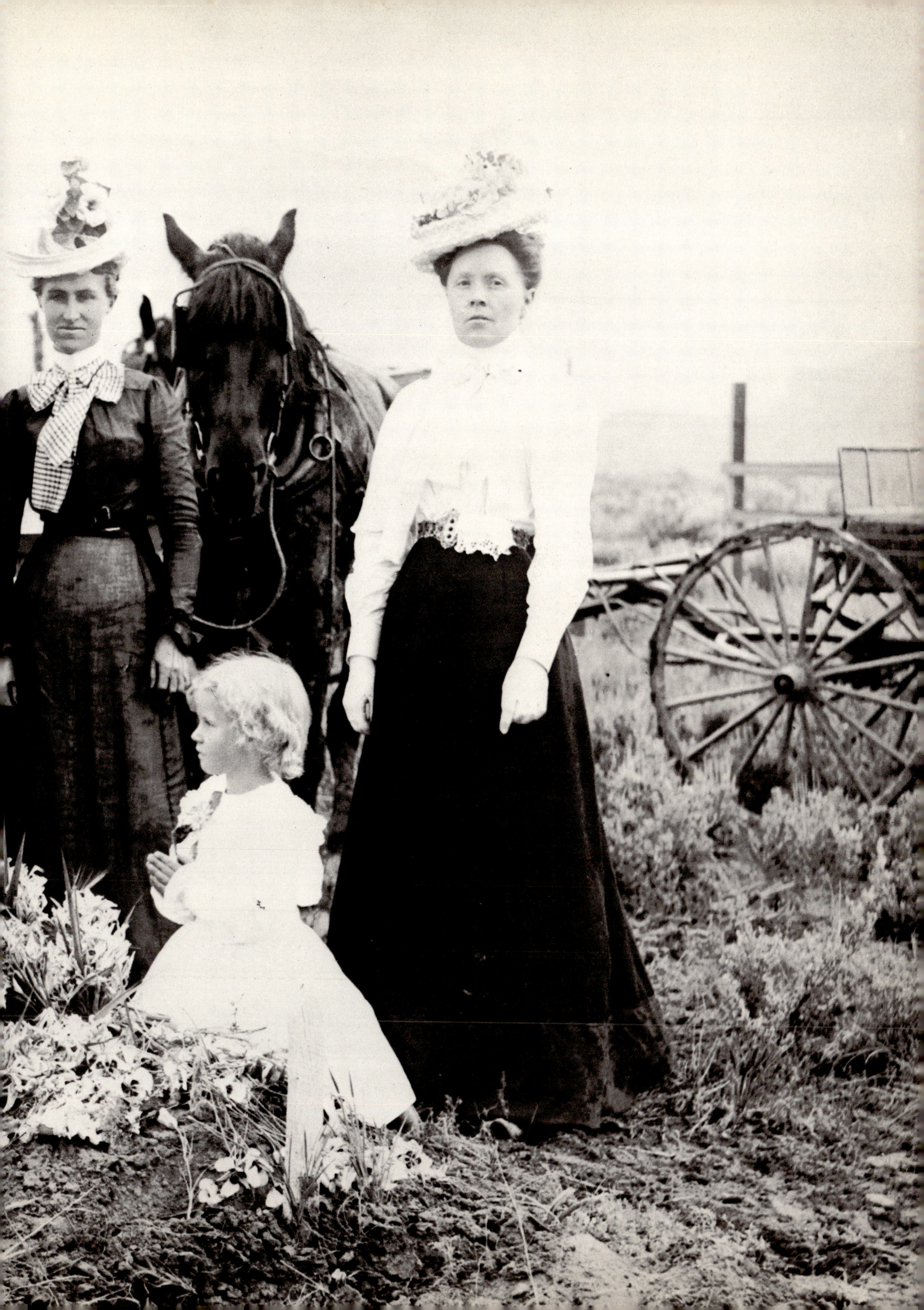

Small-town courtship was a circumspect matter, no doubt carried on with more freedom than in an earlier age but still marked by a definite code of morality. "Romance suffused the American nineties, and romance was incompatible with our quite realistic knowledge of sex," writes Henry Seidel Canby of his youth. "A thrilling imagination sometimes suggested the possibility of joining the two, but that was to be later. The girl must be won first, and won romantically...." Chaperoning the couple in the scene below is Mrs. Jeanette Bernard, an avid photography buff who lived in the far reaches of Queens on New York's Long Island, an area of farms and villages at the turn of the century. Mrs. Bernard carefully composed the picture and then had a friend click the shutter. The romantic setting for the boaters at right is the Susquehanna River near its source, Otsego Lake, in New York State. The picture was taken by Cooperstown's Putt Telfer.

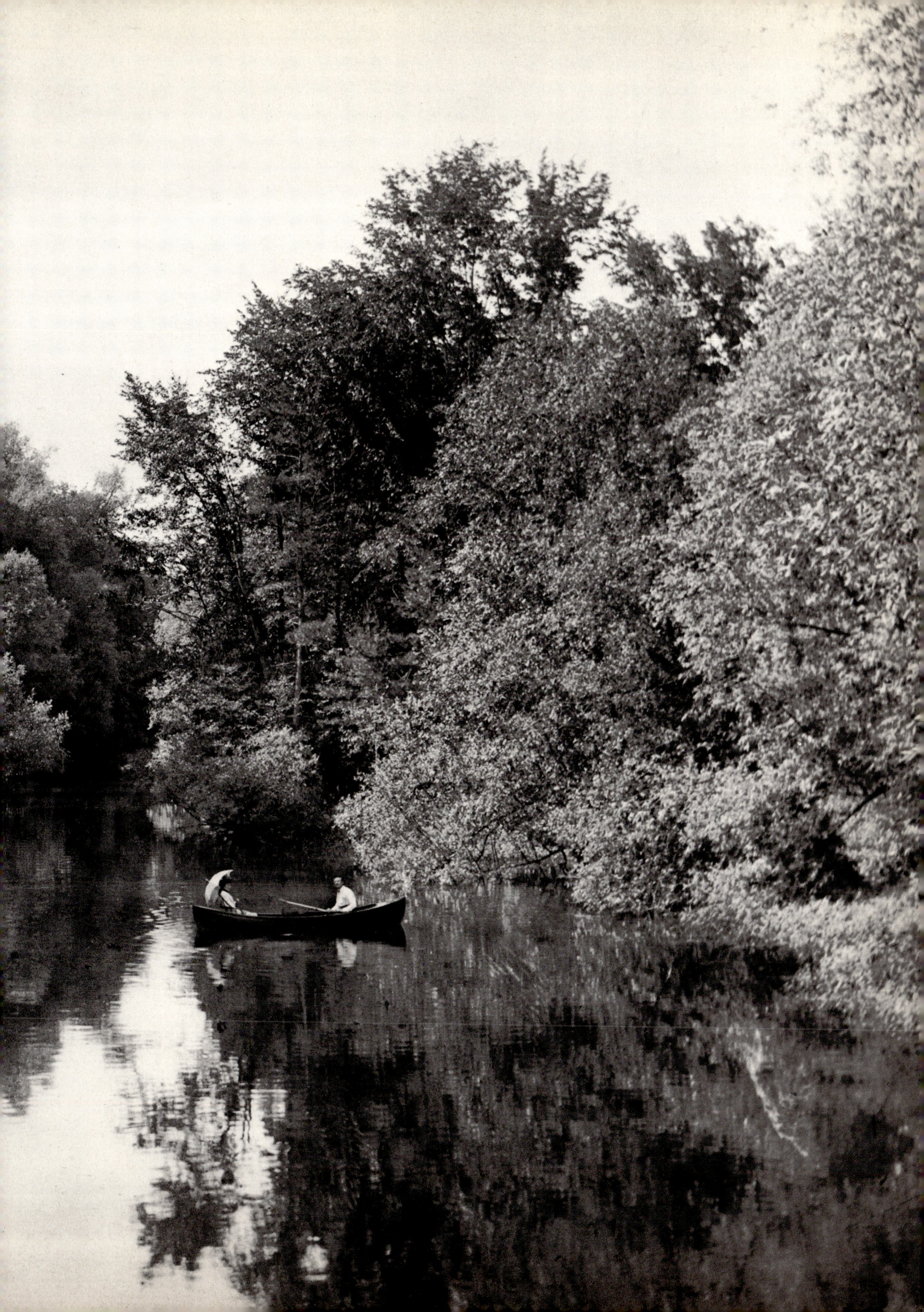

NEW YORK STATE HISTORICAL ASSOCIATION

The wedding day: usually formal, perhaps stiff, certainly ceremonious enough to be remembered and treasured. Above is the scene at a church in New Jersey, with everyone, down to the youngest spectator, dressed to the nines. At the left is the traditional disposal of the bridal bouquet, recorded by Cooperstown's Telfer in 1908. The bride is Florence Bundy and this was her family's home, at which the reception celebrating her marriage to Clermonte Tennant was held. The group at the right is identified only as the Pauley wedding party, and there is hardly a smile to be seen. The photograph was taken by J.J. Pennell at Junction City, Kansas, in 1901.

BROWN BROTHERS

OVERLEAF: The newlyweds are unidentified, but their wedding-gift display offers a handy cross section of turn-of-the-century middle-America taste. There are pitchers, platters, dishes, servers, cruets, vases, trays, tureens, and figurines, in silver, porcelain, cut glass, and a medly of "art glass"; and there are pillows and memory books and paintings dripping with Victorian sentimentality. Dr. Charles Swap took the picture in Boonville, Missouri.

KANSAS COLLECTION, KENNETH SPENCER RESEARCH LIBRARY, UNIVERSITY OF KANSAS

MISSOURI HISTORICAL SOCIETY

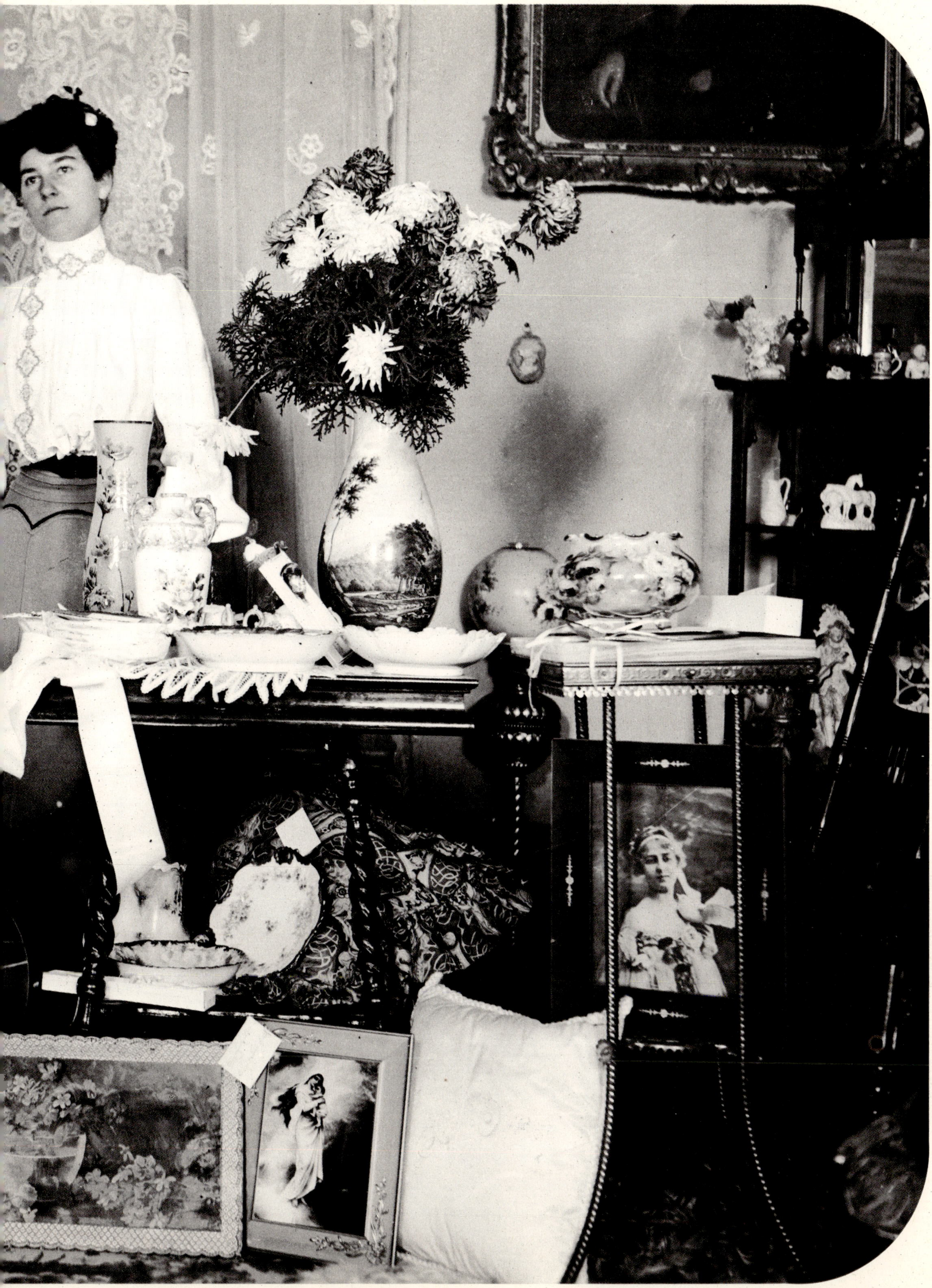

BOTH: COLLECTION OF DAVID R. PHILLIPS

100

An unknown photographer in Ashtabula, Ohio, took these evocations of parenthood about 1904. The glass-plate negatives bear the terse captions, "Alois in Tub" and "Alois with Father." Beyond that nothing is known; perhaps nothing more is needed.

CULVER PICTURES

"Many hands make light work," one of any number of old saws regularly intoned in the family circle, underlined the fact that operating a household was too large a task not to be shared. Chores were required of everyone, ranging from (as Meredith Willson noted them in *The Music Man*) pulling dandelions and pounding beefsteaks to patching the screen door and pumping water for the Saturday-night baths. At left is feeding time for the poultry inhabiting Mrs. Bernard's Long Island back yard. The garden forever needed weeding (above) and there were always some yard chores to do; Mrs. Drake took the photograph below of her husband and nephew in 1896.

CULVER PICTURES

Here are a few samples of the woman's work that was never done. Although the lady of the house is shown at the well and woodbox, these jobs were usually assigned to able-bodied sons—or at least that is the vivid recollection of a great many able-bodied sons. Washing dishes and scrubbing clothes were endless tasks, and in the average small-town home that meant hand-drawn water heated at the range, washboards, and homemade soap. By the early years of the century increasing numbers of women were turning to "store-bought" soap for personal use, but many still made their washing soap. Chansonetta Emmons took the dishwasher's picture in Maine; the Monday wash scene is by Mrs. Bernard. The other two pictures are by unknown photographers.

BOTH: BROWN BROTHERS

CULVER PICTURES

"My mother's kitchen was always astir with activity or evidence of some project," Walter O'Meara remembers. "There would be a golden sheet of noodles drying on a clean dish towel over the back of a chair. Or a small keg of shredded cabbage turning to sauerkraut in a warm corner. Or a bag of cottage cheese dripping whey into a pan. Perhaps even a crock of dandelion wine fermenting...." One of the irksome tasks for those who kept chickens was singeing; at left, Mrs. Bernard demonstrates the technique. At right, her daughter, with thimble and thread handy, shows the way to sew up the bird. The kitchen range below is operating at capacity. The pipes at the left are part of the water-heating system; below them are irons.

CULVER PICTURES

Holidays spawned community spirit, and no holiday brought people closer
than Christmas. The typical highlights were decorating the tree,
visiting, and the Christmas Eve program at church. Lewis Atherton has
described one such program, held at the Congregational church in
Algona, Iowa, in 1886. Following the invocation and songs by several of
the Sunday school classes, Atherton relates, "George Horton gave
a recitation, 'What Santa Claus Saw,' and Howard Robinson followed with
another called 'The Orphan's Christmas' . . . and the program went on
through recitations, dialogues and songs until all children had made an
appearance." Another lasting tradition was Christmas dinner (below),
where the family head did the honors and no one ever left the
table hungry. One Christmas morning about 1900, Master Syl Dankoler
(opposite) was the recipient of a good dose of the classics (the less
visible title beneath the tree is *Swiss Family Robinson*). The
motto on the bookcase—"Good Books are our Best Friends"—suggests
this family's aspirations. Harry E. Dankoler, a photographer
and journalist based in Sturgeon Bay, Wisconsin, took the picture.

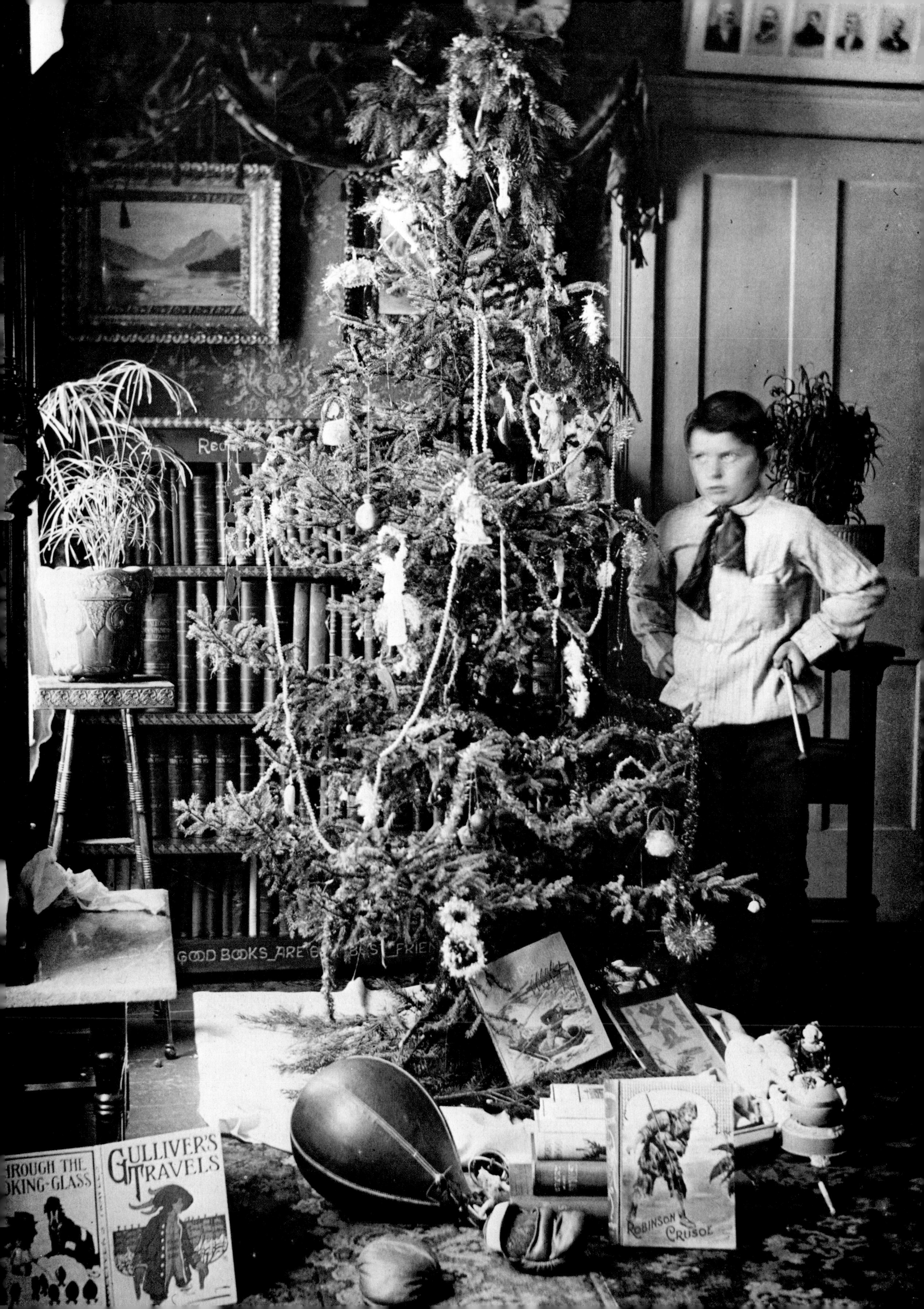
GULLIVER'S TRAVELS
ROBINSON CRUSOE

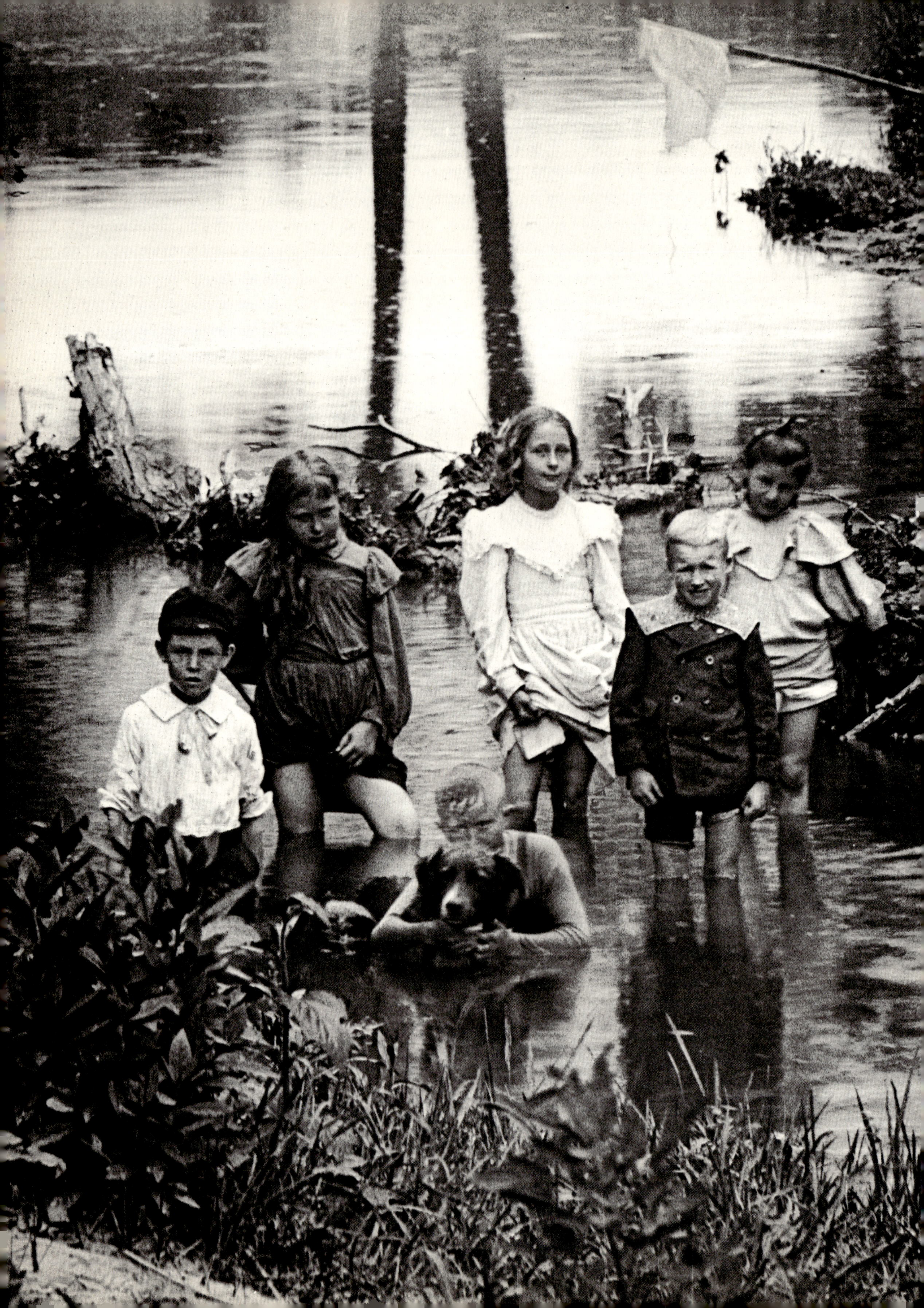

CHAPTER
4
Growing Up

The accounts and memoirs examining American small-town life in the decades that framed the turn of the century are a partisan lot. Some sing the subject's praises and others find much to criticize; the reviews are mixed. But the portions of these writings that deal only with childhood in that time and place are something else. Few memoirists can recall anything unpleasant about the experience, except for such things as Saturday night baths and paying duty calls on fearsomely forbidding relatives. Such uniformity suggests that growing up in a small town in that era was truly a happy experience.

Of course, it can be argued that childhood is a happy enough experience in *any* era. Yet there seems to be a special sense of unstained innocence that shines through many of the pictures in this chapter. The young Californians seen here, for example, pants legs rolled up and dresses hiked above the waterline, have just that quality (the occasion was a family picnic or outing in Northern California about 1900; the photographer's name is unknown). "Childhood then mirrored a peace of mind that is not to be found today," observes Civil War historian

Bruce Catton of his youth in a small Michigan town before the Great War.

One reason growing up then may have been more pleasant than it was at least for previous generations was the changed attitudes of parents toward their children. "Childhood then and there was in its period of *laissez-faire*," Henry Seidel Canby theorized in *The Age of Confidence*. In the closing decades of the nineteenth century, Canby continued, "It was the grandparents you had to watch out for. Every family had a Great-Aunt Lizzie or a Grandma Smith with a thimble for knuckles and a withering voice, while the grandfathers, when they were not affectionate, looked through children as if they were not there. Parents were by no means indulgent, yet they seemed usually to be secretly leagued with us to give the child a chance in the house. . . . He was free to make his own world, provided it did not interfere with the decorum of adult life. . . ."

This new attitude did not extend very far among the vast numbers of the urban poor, nor in most cases to those growing up on farms. There the demand for labor was still as great as it had ever been, and as soon as a child was physically able, he or she was doing the work of an adult. But it was different in the small towns. Perhaps Utopia was still out of reach, but R. L. Duffus admitted that he and his cronies in Williamstown, Vermont, comprised "the only leisure class in town."

There was nothing in the way of organized, structured recreation for the young. Parents were not required to furnish transportation for their offspring because wherever they wanted to go could be reached on foot. Parents, in fact, were not expected to involve themselves at all in children's pastimes beyond occasionally lending a helping hand for something special. The neighborhood theatrical troupe depicted on page 137, for example, surely had the expert assistance of several mothers in the making of those costumes. But that was the exception. The general rule was that children amused themselves on their own, subject only to such rules as finishing their chores first and getting home in time for supper.

As noted earlier, the chore system was essential to the functioning of the household. Keeping the woodbox stocked and the kitchen range reservoir filled were standard tasks for boys, as were the feeding of and cleaning up after any livestock the family maintained—poultry, a horse or two, perhaps a cow. Beating rugs, keeping the cistern full, filling and trimming the kerosene lamps, and cutting grass in summer and shoveling snow in winter were other regular chores. A daughter began early to carry a share of the heavy housekeeping load, participating in everything from stuffing pillows to putting up preserves. This was considered essential training for her anticipated life's role—marriage and the raising of a family in a house of her own.

Unfortunately, relatively few women have set down their recollections of small-town life seventy or eighty years ago, and so the impression is too often left that little girls' amusements were limited to dollhouses, parlor games, dress-up sessions, berry picking, and getting into the hair of their older brothers. No doubt this list is quite incomplete—William Allen White remembered a certain Dora Rector, who "commanded our respect [and] could without scandal do turns on the bar and was not ashamed if her skirt flopped over her head and showed her chaste and ruffled drawers while she hung by her legs. . . ."—but it is also true that boys had more options because they could range farther afield. (If it was then a man's world, perhaps it was a boy's world as well.) For them, running a trap line was not uncommon, nor was hunting for those lucky enough to have received a single-shot .22 from a generous uncle or earned one selling magazines. Kite-flying and fishing and the carefully structured game of marbles were universal. A good deal of time was spent simply wandering down to the quarry or searching for hickory nuts and buckeyes in the woods and for fresh windfalls in the orchard. But there was as well a great deal to see and do on Main Street itself. As a boy in Pine Grove, Pennsylvania, Conrad Richter relished watching the craftsmen at the wheelwright's, playing in the lumberyard, and, best of all, visiting the blacksmith's to marvel at the flying sparks, pump the bellows, and witness special events; "news that a kicking or a killer horse was to be put in the stocks to be shod spread like wildfire over the neighborhood and spectators appeared like locusts out of the ground . . . ," he reported.

During his Kansas boyhood William Allen White commandeered a corner of the woodshed to store what he termed the tools of his trade—"a thick piece of glass that was used for scraping and polishing cowhorns; a drawknife; skates with runners, rubbed with bacon rind to keep away rust; bits of iron that had no use but were potentially of extreme value . . . ; a rawhide quirt—an eight-strand, square-braided whip of my own construction, a priceless treasure; [and] rows and ranks of cigar boxes filled with nails, screws, tops, marbles, and Heaven only knows what of the wampum of boyhood."

To this typical list might be added a few additional pieces of sports equipment: a homemade and constantly unwinding baseball and a bat contrived from a wagon tongue or an axe handle; a bow and arrows, also homemade; an iron-runnered sled; perhaps mail-order boxing gloves ($1.10 for two pairs). Basketball was too new a sport to have yet received widespread attention; and football, although college results were avidly followed, was seldom played because of the equipment cost.

All things considered, it was very much a Tom Sawyerish sort of world. Walter O'Meara explains how he and his friends managed to pass the days of summer: "We made slip-whistles from green willow twigs, red ink from a little forest flower whose name I do not know, wintergreen tea (and drank it cold), little pipes from acorns and a bit of straw. We played mumblety-peg, one old cat, and duck-on-the-rock. We walked fences, whittled wooden chains (seldom successfully), caught frogs and tadpoles, flushed out gophers, imprisoned fireflies under a jelly glass, searched for four-leaf clovers. Even less productively we spent idle hours watching water bugs skate on the glassy surface of a still pond or a hawk wheeling in the pale summer sky...."

The one crimp in this pleasing life-style was school. The actual details of the learning process are recalled hazily if at all by most memoirists, probably because the curriculum of the average small-town school system was far from intellectually challenging. "We got discipline of the kind that teaches to do it now and don't ask foolish questions," writes Canby; "we got reading and reciting; and for the rest of the time were inflated with the rapidly multiplying volume of things to know which was to leave most of us with cluttered minds and weakened judgment." What is remembered most about school includes the uncomfortable desks, dipping pigtails in inkwells, the awkward giving and getting of Valentines, scraped knees at recess, and the ritual challenge to every new kid by the school bully. A few endured high school and escaped to college; others were lucky enough to live in a town with a library, and to discover it; but most entered the mainstream of life with little more than basic reading, 'riting, and 'rithmetic.

The two holidays most cherished by the younger generation were, not surprisingly, Halloween and the Fourth of July. On Halloween night there was no trick-or-treating. Rather it was a case (so the perpetrators liked to believe) of utterly terrorizing the town. This process, according to O'Meara, included ringing doorbells, peppering houses with peashooters, and the use of the fiendish ticktack—a kind of homemade top featuring a notched spool that raised a clatter against windowglass when set spinning on the sill. Older boys engaged in more mature depredations, such as splintering picket fences, pilfering gates, knocking over privies and woodpiles, and removing buggies or livestock to unlikely places. The town constable was always kept busy on Halloween. Ruminating on such behavior in his Michigan hometown, Bruce Catton comments, "I have never had any trouble understanding the miseries which General Sherman's army inflicted on the people of Georgia in 1864; it simply turned its small-town rowdies loose. They had their Halloween in broad daylight with full government approval, and I am sure they enjoyed it...."

At the top of the list was the Glorious Fourth. There were skyrockets and torpedoes and salutes of various calibres to fire off, a high proportion of which were aimed vengefully at the school principal's front porch, the crabby old maid's house down the street, and similar strategic targets. And there was a staggering amount of activity to take in. Western historian David Lavender grew up in the tough Colorado mining town of Telluride, and while the Fourth in Telluride had certain unique features all its own, its observance had much in common with small towns across the nation. "The celebrations, as I remember them through a boy's eyes," writes Lavender, "were magnificent beyond telling. Parades in the morning—brass bands, marching miners, fire engines buried in crepe paper, fraternal orders in uniform, princesses on wagons piled with evergreens and festooned by blue-and-white columbines. Dogs and firecrackers.... Rock-drilling teams struggling to punch, within a specified time, the deepest hole into a ten-ton block of granite set on a platform in the middle of Colorado Avenue.... Footracers in spangled tights. Tug-of-war teams, heaving on either end of a rope. Hose teams blasting each other off their feet with heads of ice water that had dropped from the peaktops...."

All in all, these were good years in which to be young. Days were bright and hopes for the future were high. R. L. Duffus remembered that at the age of ten in 1898 the only thing he wanted from life was to be like Old Man Webb, an engineer on the Central Vermont Railroad: "to sit in a cab with my hand on the throttle, and chew tobacco and spit out the window, and maybe wave at a group of admiring boys beside the right of way—maybe, maybe, maybe—the western sky was bright with maybes...."

Whether they liked it or not, there came a time when
most every boy and girl was led off to the town photographer's
for a portrait. The photographer unrolled a tasteful
backdrop and bent to the effort of persuading the subject to
stand still and look natural enough that the parents
could be talked into buying the picture. Here are two
entirely successful efforts. We do not know the names of the
polite boys below, but one J. E. Frazier of Eagle Bend,
Minnesota, took their portrait. The lovely sisters opposite
are Altana (left) and Esther Willis of Cooperstown,
New York, who were taken to Putt Telfer's studio in 1905.

AMERICAN HERITAGE COLLECTION

NEW YORK STATE HISTORICAL ASSOCIATION

115

The charmer above riding her fancy rocking horse was the youngest daughter of Isabel Drake, who photographed her in 1890 at the family's summer place on Keuka Lake in New York State. An amateur photographer, Elmer G. Jacobs, persuaded the equally charming young lady on the facing page to pose for him with her teddy bear and all her favorite dolls. The scene is Grafton, New York, around 1910.

COLLECTION OF MRS. JOSEPH MAHONEY

OVERLEAF: A feature of Dublin, New Hampshire's, annual horse show was the contest for the best-decorated carriage. Here is one of the entries, photographed about 1903 by Henry D. Allison. A lifelong Dubliner, Allison ran a general store, sold real estate, and served as postmaster and selectman when not taking pictures. We know neither the girl's name nor if she won, but we like to think she did.

COLLECTION OF ELLIOT S. ALLISON

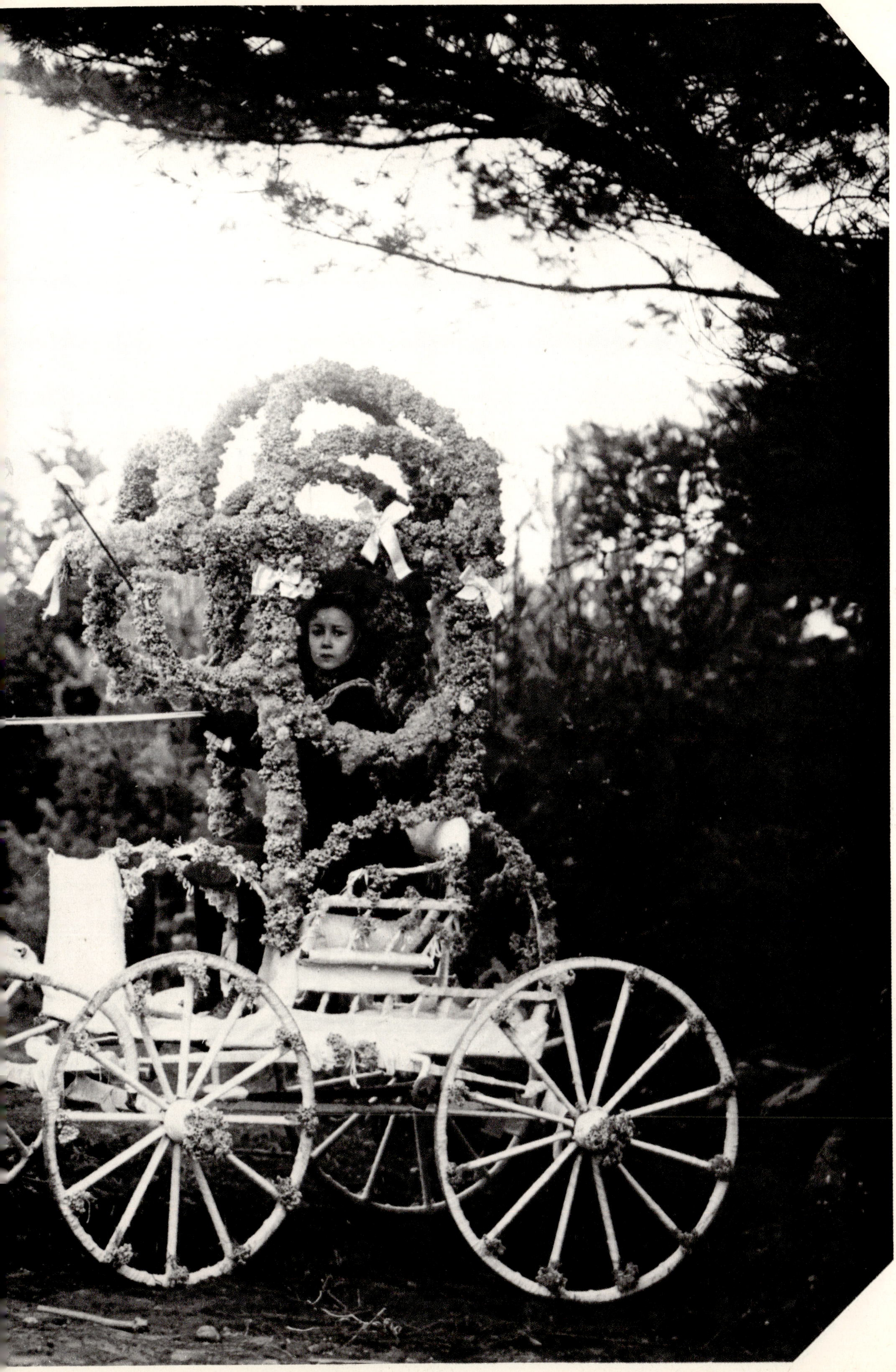

MASSILLON MUSEUM

AMERICAN HERITAGE COLLECTION

120

It has never taken very much to amuse kids. The bubble-blowers are another of the character studies made by Belle Johnson of Monroe City, Missouri. Although it is a studio setting the girls look entirely natural, and on the back of the print she sent to a photographer friend, Miss Belle wrote with pride, "Prize picture at International Contest at Paris, France, 1905." Kids have been balance-walking on railroad tracks probably from the day Robert L. Stevens spiked down his first section of T-rail in 1830; the practitioners shown here are daughters of Isabel Drake, who photographed them at the depot in Palmyra, New York, in 1890. The marvelously spontaneous picture below was taken by Nebraskan Frederick B. Humphrey. What probably set Humphrey's subjects off is the fact that the card on the left has put his shoes on the wrong feet.

NEBRASKA STATE HISTORICAL SOCIETY

CULVER PICTURES

122

Pets were an integral part of growing up. The young pet lovers portrayed here do not require amplifying descriptions, but for the record, they were from (left to right) New York, Vermont, and Illinois. Every small town was overrun with pets of great variety and indifferent ancestry. For example, Bruce Catton and his brother shared their Michigan boyhood with a dog named Bobby. "Bobby was a mongrel," Catton admits, "largely collie in origin, and she had been the runt of the litter. She never attained more than two thirds of the size proper for a dog of her ancestry, and she had been born with a tail that was bushy enough but was only about eight inches long. . . ." Bobby was also on the timid side (on every Fourth of July she retired to the woodshed until the last celebrant ran out of firecrackers) and was sorely tried by the family tomcat, but such minor faults mattered not at all—and these faces show why.

COLLECTION OF MELVIN ADELGLASS

STATE HISTORICAL SOCIETY OF WISCONSIN

PHOTOGRAPHIC ARCHIVES, UNIVERSITY OF LOUISVILLE

"The editor of this paper desires to buy a horse," wrote William Allen White in his Emporia *Gazette* in 1906. Style and speed were not essential; what was wanted, he explained, was a gentle horse "of the kind that children can use to put a teeter-totter across." These three horses would surely have qualified. Above is patient Billy, photographed in Boonville, Missouri, by Dr. Charles Swap. George H. Dabbs of Morgantown, Kentucky, took the other pictures. At the left is young Allie Monroe Mauzy, and below, "a bunch of Morgantown Roses" (as Dabbs described them).

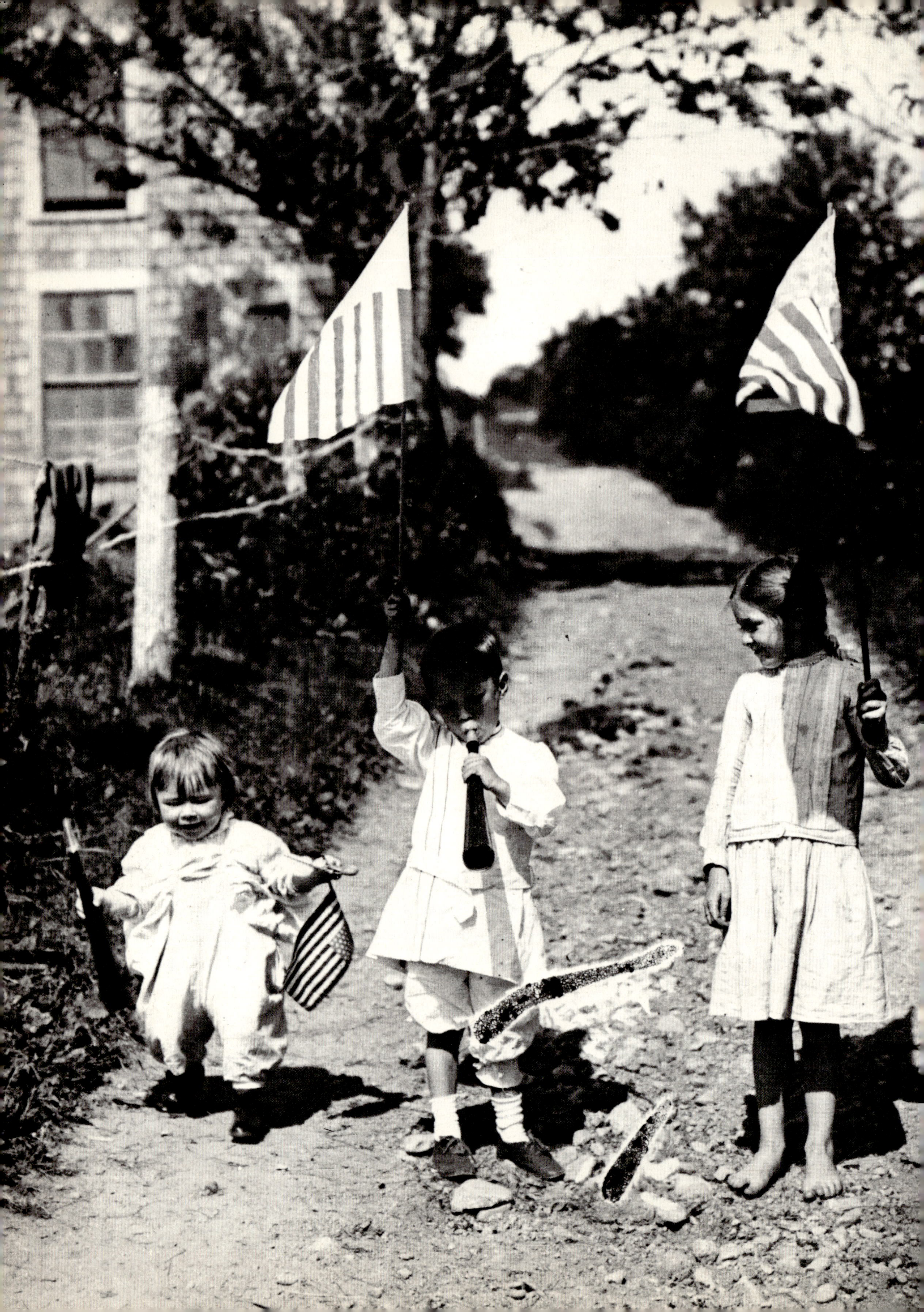

The highlight of summer was of course the Glorious Fourth. The boys at left are too fancied-up for the day; perhaps they were to take part in the patriotic observances at the town park. The young ladies below "starred" in a special Fourth of July ball game at Black River Falls, Wisconsin. The celebrants on the facing page were photographed in Kingfield, Maine, by Chansonetta Stanley Emmons. She used a dry-plate photographic process invented in 1880 by her twin brothers, F.E. and F.O. Stanley, who later were to come up with the celebrated Steamer.

OVERLEAF: These intent young readers no doubt earned at least free admissions to the show for posing for the 101 Ranch's PR man. On this occasion the famous wild West troupe was playing at home in Ponca City, Oklahoma.

MILLER BROTHERS
BIG ROUND-UP OF THOUSANDS OF LONG HORNED STEERS
WILD
101
REAL
RANCH
101 RANCH REAL WILD WEST
101 RANCH REAL WILD WEST
PONCA CITY 29

WEST SHOW
29
WILD WEST
ER
EXPERT DIVERSIFIED FARMING PRIZE HAMPSHIRE HOGS
101 RANCH
AUTO POLO
HOME AND HEADQUARTERS OF
"WHITE HOUSE" THE MILLER BROTHERS
SEAT OF FAMOUS
PONCA INDIAN

KANSAS COLLECTION, KENNETH SPENCER RESEARCH LIBRARY, UNIVERSITY OF KANSAS

Hunting and fishing were youthful pastimes enjoyed in every part of the country, and sometimes a bit of cash could result. The rabbit hunters below, photographed in Missouri, posed happily at a local meat dealer's. How much he paid them is not known. On the opposite page, Master Gilbert Emick of Junction City, Kansas, aims his $1 Brownie at two friends and the catch they have taken from the Smoky Hill River. Presumably J. J. Pennell, who made this glass-plate picture of the snapshot session in 1902, was the one who persuaded the boys to go home and put on their Sunday suits in honor of the occasion; they surely did not go fishing dressed like that.

CHARLES PHELPS CUSHING

Snowman-building is a timeless practice, but there was one advantage to the game at the turn of the century: the bowler hat was in, and without question a snowman looks best in a bowler. The scene below was photographed by Isabel Drake at Palmyra, New York, in 1907. Another cold-weather practice was sugaring off, and at the right is a tableaux on the subject, carefully staged by photographer Wills White of Bennington, Vermont. The young experts demonstrate the gathering of sap from the spiles, the use of a wooden collection tub, and the boiling of sap in an iron kettle. As the axman keeps the firewood coming, his friend on the sled samples finished maple syrup or sugar. The stuffed squirrel and owl (right) add the finishing touch to the composition.

AMERICAN HERITAGE COLLECTION

COLLECTION OF ROBERT L. WEICHERT

STATE HISTORICAL SOCIETY OF WISCONSIN

COLLECTION OF DAVID R. PHILLIPS

"In some ways winter was the most exciting season of all, especially during the first few weeks," recalls Bruce Catton. "After that it began to seem endless, and by the middle of February we began to feel as if we had been frozen in forever, but at first it was fun." The skiers at left, photographed about 1910 at Stoughton, Wisconsin, were still at the fun stage. Their skis were probably turned out by the local carpenter, they have neither poles nor special outfits, and their bindings were simply leather or rope loops; but the slope does not appear to be very risky. Skating was a more common winter sport. Below is a race at Saranac Lake, New York, in the 1890's.

PHOTOGRAPHIC ARCHIVES, UNIVERSITY OF LOUISVILLE

The better element in town took the lead in promoting the idea of children's parties. Someone (it is not clear who) at the festive table above was celebrating a fourth birthday. Halloween was another occasion for party-going and such games as bobbing for apples (below right). But the real fun was in dressing up and giving a play. The thespians opposite, posing in 1915 in a back yard in Massillon, Ohio, staged shows in neighborhood barns and playhouses.

OVERLEAF: An institution that has disappeared from the American scene is the county orphanage, but early in the century it was very much in evidence. This is Christmas time about 1909, and the two ladies standing in the back of the French-built Hotchkiss are conducting the annual ritual of gift-giving at the local orphans' home.

BROWN BROTHERS

136

MASSILLON MUSEUM

BETTMANN ARCHIVE

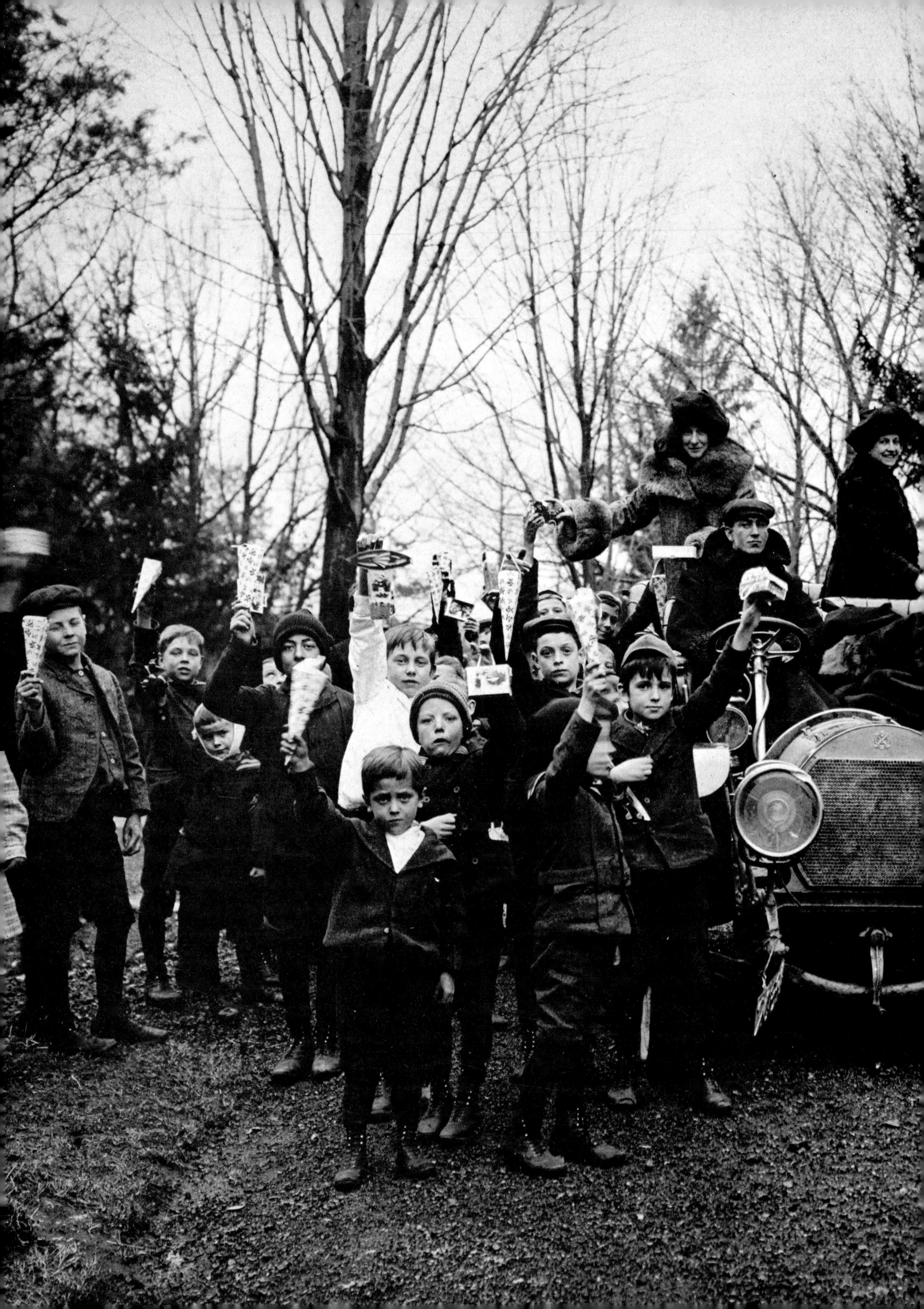

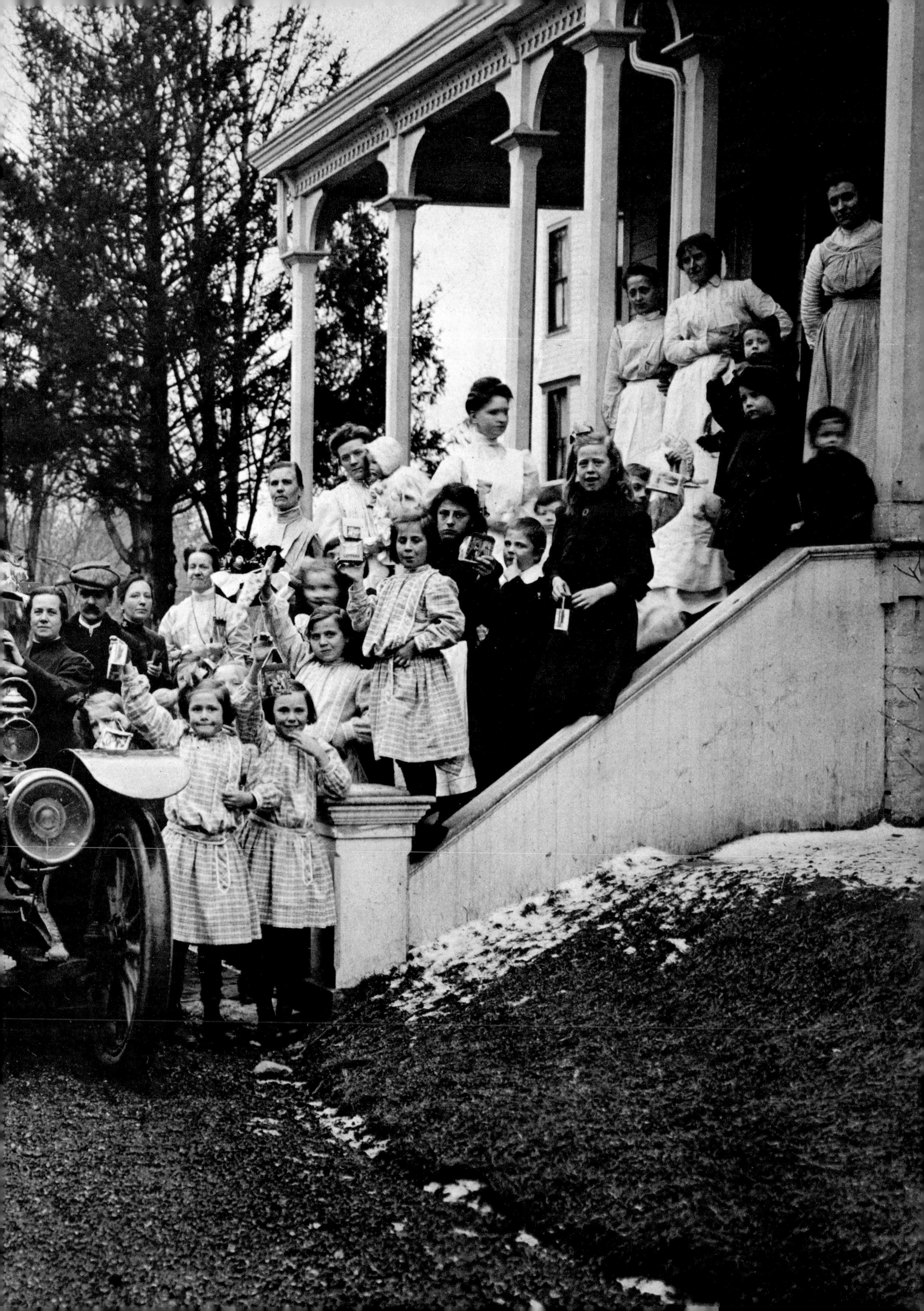

STATE HISTORICAL SOCIETY OF WISCONSIN

CULVER PICTURES

American public education was entering a yeasty period at the turn of the century, but reforms and improvements were slow to trickle down to small-town schools. Generally, they continued their devotion to the practical: the three R's, learned by rote and discipline. The teaching profession was low-paying and poorly regarded (schoolmarms, however, were highly regarded as matrimonial prospects) and turnover was rapid. The teacher below appears to be in full charge of her Hoosier classroom. The decorations and the blackboard drawings suggest that the occasion for the picture, which dates from the mid-1890's, was Columbus Day observances. The maypole scene at the left was photographed in the schoolyard in River Grove, Illinois, in 1900 a village of some 330, outside Chicago. The students below left are doing their exercising inside the classroom. This is Kingfield, Maine, photographed by Chansonetta Emmons.

INDIANA HISTORICAL SOCIETY LIBRARY

One of a town photographer's springtime rituals was the taking of class pictures. Whoever took the one above managed to get everybody's attention—possibly because the teacher left her bell on the railing and stood behind the camera. These upper elementary students pose on the front steps of their school in Melrose, Massachusetts. One October day in 1903 William L. Bennett set up his camera on the Union School playground in Navarre, Ohio, and (it may be assumed) called out, "Anybody want to have his picture taken?" At right is the result.

OVERLEAF: School is over, it is summer (July, 1896), and this time Bennett's camera is aimed at the long-abandoned Ohio and Erie Canal near Navarre. Here is the old swimming hole of song and story, precisely as nostalgia has pictured it.

MASSILLON MUSEUM

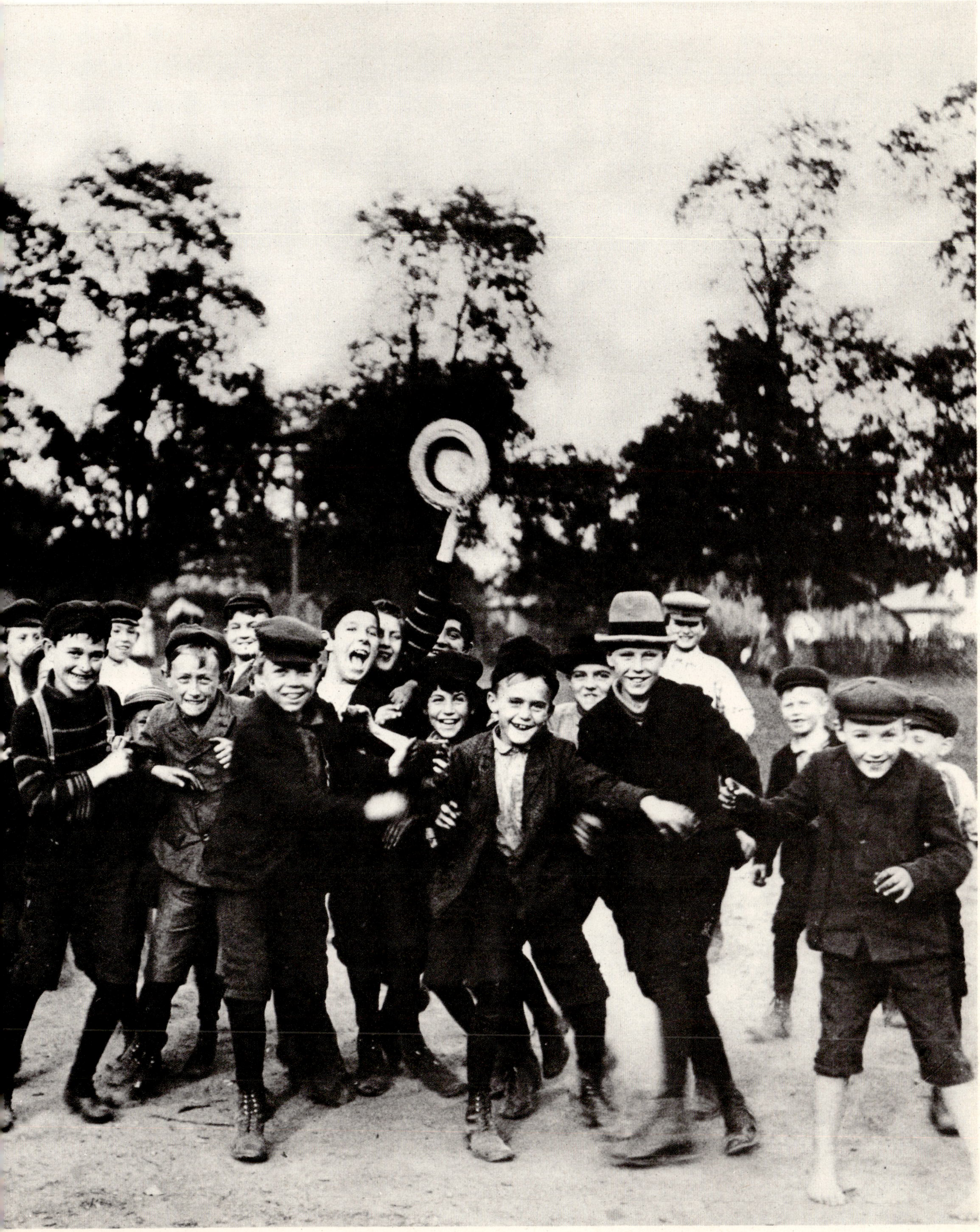

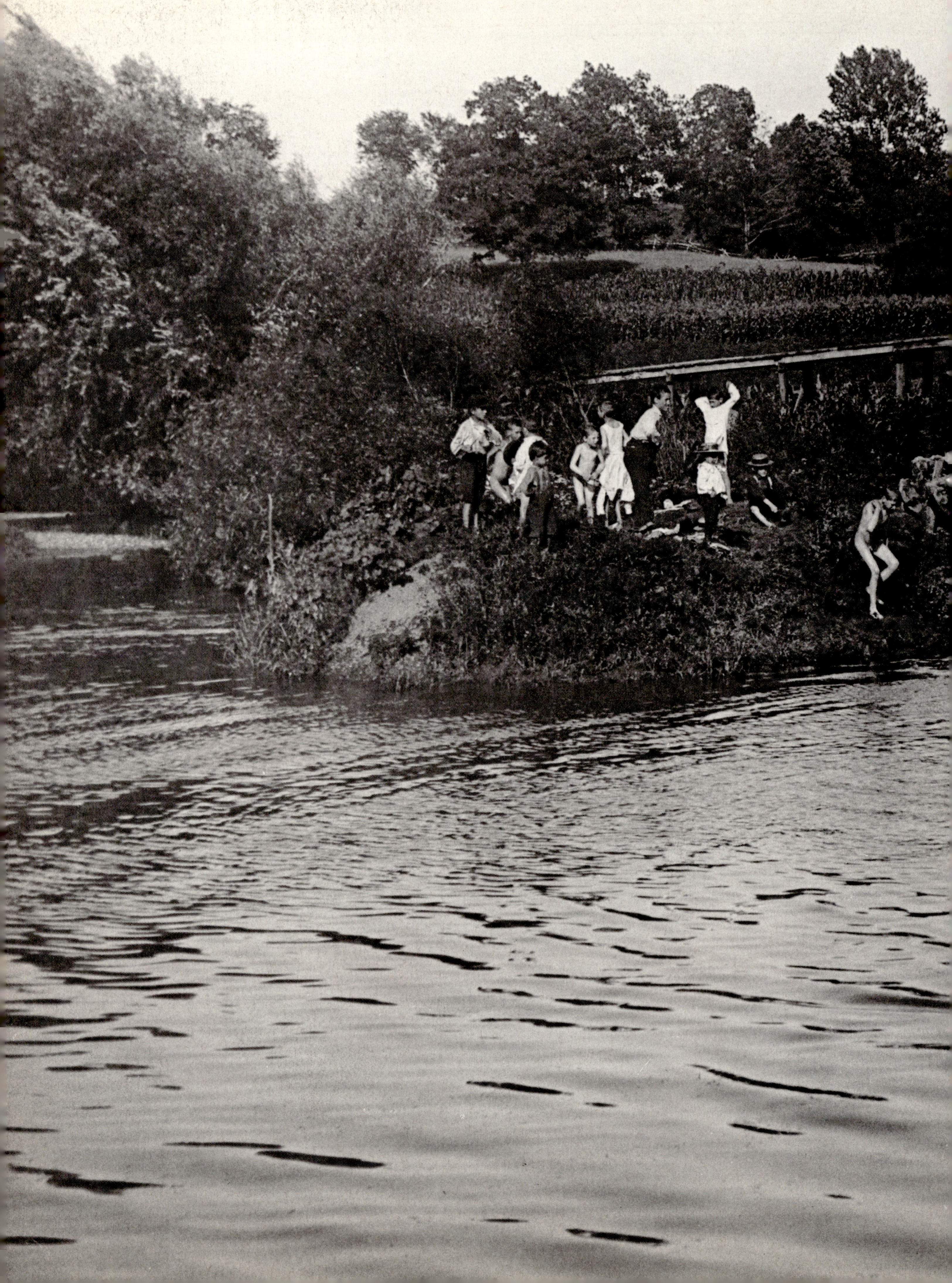

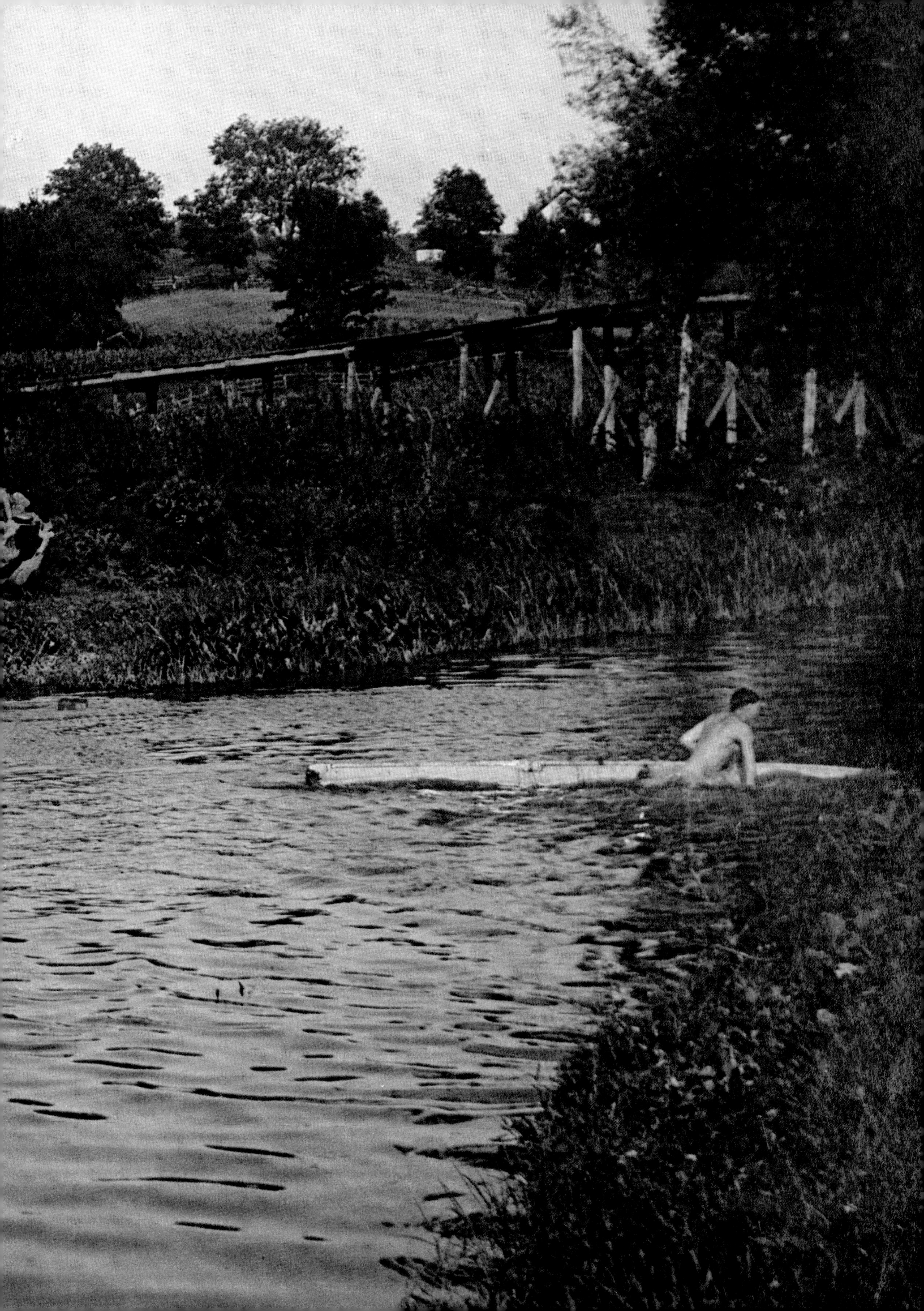

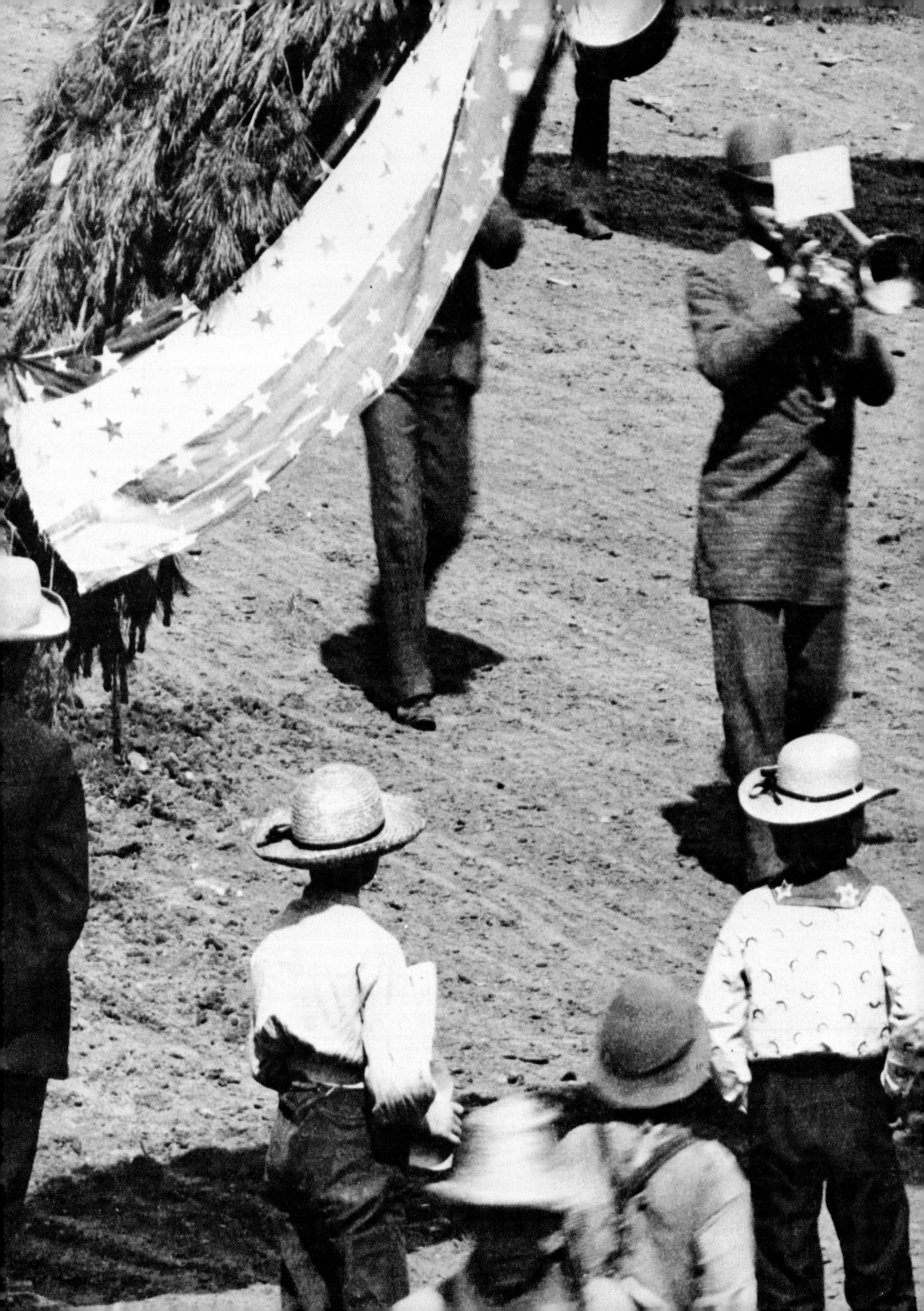

CHAPTER
5
Life's Small Pleasures

Parade-watching ranked high on a six- or seven-year-old's scale of life's small pleasures, and Decoration Day—as Memorial Day was invariably called—was the occasion for one of the grandest parades on the small-town calendar. This is May 30, 1890, in Black River Falls, Wisconsin, as seen through Charles Van Schaick's camera. Amidst flags and bunting and the traditional evergreen garlands, the town band sets the pace down Main Street, trailed by dignitaries in carriages, a patriotic float, and the blue ranks of the Grand Army of the Republic. (In the Southern states ex-Confederates marched to a different drum on other days.) Typically, the procession made its way to the town cemetery for readings of the Gettysburg Address and Will Carleton's poem "Cover Them Over with Beautiful Flowers" and the decorating of the soldiers' graves with wreaths or sprigs of evergreen. The day's observances concluded in the town park or around the bandstand with what one Illinois editor described as "elocutionary entertainment."

The Civil War veterans played an important role in

the small town's scheme of things, and Decoration Day was the high point of their year. William Allen White recalled his father grumbling that the marching ranks included "a lot of damn bounty jumpers," but his view may have been colored by his status as a lonely Democrat in a town full of Republicans who waved the bloody shirt. More commonly the old soldiers were regarded as pillars of the community—"the keepers of its patriotic traditions, the living embodiment, so to speak, of what it most deeply believed about the nation's greatness and high destiny," as Bruce Catton phrased it.

In addition to the standard holiday observances, there were celebrations of special events peculiar to certain places or regions—the birthday of a distinguished local historical figure, or the anniversary of a town's founding, for two examples. Educator Gerard E. Jensen recounted one such highlight of his boyhood in Norwich, Connecticut—the annual Thanksgiving barrel-burning. "Contending gangs of boys of all ages worked for long months preceding the great day, gathering barrels and hiding them away in cellars and barns until they should be wanted for burning," Jensen wrote. "We begged, stole, and forcibly took from other boys, in the open or under concealment of darkness. . . . The gangs gathered in literally *all* the wooden barrels in the city, including those in current use for ashes and trash in every family." On the appointed day tall pyramids of barrels rose across the countryside, and at nightfall, after the traditional Thanksgiving feast, the pyres were touched off as the whole town watched. "We gathered in a circle around our fire, absorbed for the moment in its glory. . . . Norwich, being a city on several hills, lit its Jail Hill barrels last, and those in the valleys first, and one by one the columns of flame began to illuminate Lanman Hill, Plain Hill, Wawecus Hill. The sky was lurid with orange flames and smoke for a good hour—then the illumination began to die down and all that remained were heaps of red charcoal that glowed all night and still smouldered in the early morning of the next day."

One of the decisive facts about American small-town society was that so many of its pleasures were necessarily self-generated. As a result, almost any entertainment that arrived from the outside world was certain to receive a welcome. The scruffiest medicine-show barker peddling snake-oil nostrums for female weakness and lost manhood was assured of drawing a crowd. A carnival of the sort that Solomon Butcher photographed in Kearney, Nebraska (pages 182–183), would take over a town for several days and provide memories and gossip for several weeks. Most exciting of all was circus day, when exotica from the four corners of the earth, previously experienced only in the imagination, came to life. Walter O'Meara describes the beginning of such a day when the Walter L. Main show arrived in Cloquet, Minnesota.

"It would still be dark when we arrived at the railroad siding," O'Meara writes. "Flaring gasoline torches cast wild shadows over a scene of murky chaos; shouting roustabouts ducking in and out of the lighted areas; strange animal cries and grunts; the monstrous forms of elephants looming in the darkness . . . ; cages and ornate wagons lumbering down the ramps from flatcars; a mob of people from another world milling about in the pre-dawn half-light. . . ." He never had the privilege of watering the elephants, O'Meara remembers, but one year he did gain boasting rights among his peers by wearing a red fez and riding a camel (admittedly a small camel) in the circus parade.

Like so many other characteristics of small-town living, most of life's pleasures were simple and local and more or less homemade—but no less pleasurable for all that. At the turn of the century, people went for walks and buggy rides and bicycle tours; they fished and camped out and swam in nearby lakes of astonishing pureness. In wintertime they ice skated and bobsledded and a few even tried iceboating. All of this kind of activity was undertaken without undue strain or pressure and usually close to home, with the emphasis on companionship. Relations between the sexes could hardly be considered to have reached a state of grace in that era, but there was one quality worth noting. "One met one's girl," wrote Henry Seidel Canby, "not in the transitoriness of a weekend, or at the end of three hundred miles of auto road, but for long acquaintance. She would be there and you would be there next week, next year. She was one of a family, and that family part of a community which was yours. She carried with her the sanctions and the refusals of Society."

Except for such occasions as circus day, the average small town endured an isolation difficult to conceive in an age that leans so heavily as ours on radio, television, motion pictures, and the automobile for entertainment. It comes as no surprise, then, to report that the benches down at the depot were always occupied when the 5:15 accommodation pulled in or that the whistle of an arriving steamer attracted a crowd to the wharf or that the columns of the weekly paper were eagerly scanned for the "latest" news from the capital downstate and from faraway Washington. Sets of stereograph views and magic lantern slides revealing the varied wonders of California "exhibited in a most striking manner" or the picturesque habits of the distant Danes were to be found in nearly every parlor.

In his thoughtfully analytical *Main Street on the*

Middle Border (1954), Lewis Atherton developed considerable evidence that small towns—at least Midwestern small towns—were not the cultural deserts that Edgar Lee Masters and Sinclair Lewis and other debunkers had suggested. Referring to the central character in Lewis' *Main Street,* Atherton observes that "any balanced portrayal will show that artists and professional people who were born in midwestern country towns obtained encouragement and even inspiration from the same people who supposedly defeated Carol Kennicott," and he goes on to point out the intellectual incentives acknowledged by such small-towners as William Allen White, Thomas Hart Benton, Hamlin Garland, and Sherwood Anderson.

Without doubt, attempts at cultural uplift were sometimes more pathetic than successful, but this was as much a symptom of the era as of the place. The photograph of the matronly Vermont *artistes* on page 150 is humorous to our eyes, yet equally funny pictures of home-grown talent of the period are to be found in big-city archives from New York to San Francisco—the same rapt, draped poses, the same hyperbolic playbills as the one quoted in the caption. Americans of all stations and persuasions were seeking to better themselves in the turn-of-the-century period, and in the isolated small-town environment the wonder is not that they frequently failed but that they succeeded as often as they did. In a setting where the useful and the practical came first out of necessity, the number of libraries, "opera houses," lyceum associations, theater groups, and musical societies is astonishing. "A combination of ambitious professional entertainers and culturally inspired local citizens stood ready to promote 'higher' artistic and intellectual standards," Atherton concluded. "The rank-and-file residents of Main Street thus had little reason to consider their environment either barren or sterile."

The better element and the more imaginative among the middle class increasingly favored summer junkets to great wooden hotels in the mountains or rustic cabins tucked under the pines bordering a lake. Isabel Walker Drake, camera in hand, annually journeyed with her family to Drake Point on New York's Keuka Lake to spend what her picture albums (pages 172–173) suggest was a summer idyll. Yet the stay-at-homes—the vast majority of a town's population—were seldom stumped for summer pleasures.

Their choice of spectator sports, however, was limited. Horse racing at the many local tracks drew the largest crowds at the turn of the century, with trotters and pacers predominating over saddle horses (in *The Music Man* Prof. Harold Hill rouses his Iowa audience to indignation when he asks it to imagine a "stuck-up jockey boy" mounted on the famous pacer Dan Patch). The only other spectator sport of significance was baseball. Town teams tended to be casually organized, with informal schedules, no accommodations for spectators, and —unless a local merchant could be persuaded to underwrite the team—pick-up uniforms. Yet rivalries with neighboring towns could be fierce, and local papers carried charges of suborning umpires, inserting "professional" ringers in line-ups, and attempts by hometown fans to distract or intimidate visiting players. The town team in Benzonia, Michigan, where Bruce Catton grew up, compiled a most dismal record, a fact that puzzled Catton and his young cronies. The Benzonia squad, he writes, "did not chew tobacco or use triple-jointed swear words the way their opponents did, and if there was any justice they would not get licked so regularly. Apparently there was no justice. . . ."

Homemade entertainment called for a certain amount of organization, and social groupings flourished in even the smallest hamlet. Church socials and fairs were regular occurrences. Volunteer firemen were always very much in the thick of a town's social life, highlighting community events with hose-cart races and water-pumping contests, and their gleaming fire apparatus was vital to the success of any parade. Fraternal lodges were numerous and popular, with the Odd Fellows, the Masons and their Eastern Star auxiliary, and the Woodmen (an order stressing insurance programs) among the most prominent. In addition to supporting the ceremonies on Arbor Day, Decoration Day, the Glorious Fourth, and various other special occasions, lodges sponsored a wide miscellany of picnics, hay rides, dances, and outings.

Here is how Walter O'Meara remembers one of those summer Sunday afternoons at Chub Lake a half-dozen or so miles south of town: "Perhaps the Odd Fellows or the Sons of St. Olaf would be holding an outing, complete with a small band and a barrel of beer, and huge soda-fountain-size freezers of ice cream for the kids. It was all quite decorous and circumspect, the ladies twirling their parasols and gossiping or fussing with the refreshments, the men pitching horseshoes or just looking important and amused, the kids frolicking in the shallow water, young couples strolling off toward the pines." Reviewing the scene in his mind's eye, O'Meara compares it to a Renoir painting and admits that perhaps the passing years have romanticized the memory. Perhaps. Yet in countless living memories there are strikingly similar recollections of relaxed Sunday afternoons by the lake in a time less complicated and in a world more slowly paced.

The Queens of the Sea starred in *Kirmess*, a fund-raising carnival billed as the social event of the 1893 season in Burlington, Vermont. The show, backed by the Odd Fellows and the Women's Auxiliary of the Y.M.C.A., ran for eight performances in Howard's Opera House. Such graces as these rendered Scenes from Fairyland, Refined Specialties, and Beautiful Drills from Every Nation, and each act was bathed in the "changing colors of the calcium light."

WILBUR COLLECTION, UNIVERSITY OF VERMONT LIBRARY

The volunteer firemen formed one of the more socially active groups in any town. These smoke-eaters from Redwood City, California, are outfitted for pulling their hose cart in races against rival companies. The gent in the handlebar mustache in the middle row is Chief Joe Winter; among his compatriots are a grocery clerk, a room clerk, and the county clerk. The hose nozzle is entrusted to Harry Louie of the town's building and loan; at lower right is a spanner.

STATE HISTORICAL SOCIETY OF WISCONSIN

A strong impulse for cultural expression appeared in communities populated by newly arrived immigrant groups, particularly in the upper Midwest. The Moscow, Wisconsin, Library Association carefully arranged itself by sex and status for Andrew Dahl's camera. Exhorted "Forward!" by their banner, these Norwegians were seeking self-improvement, and all their symbols (book, busts, globe, microscope) are clear enough, except for the stuffed waterfowl.

MINNESOTA HISTORICAL SOCIETY

SOLOMON D. BUTCHER COLLECTION, NEBRASKA STATE HISTORICAL SOCIETY

The supreme symbol of the small-town appetite for cultural uplift was the traveling Chautauqua. About 1910 Solomon Butcher photographed the citizens of Kearney, Nebraska, crowding into the tent of one such show, perhaps for a lecture on character building or a panegyric to "red-blooded Christianity." These tent shows were spinoffs—some sanctioned, many not—of the celebrated Chautauqua Institution in New York State, founded by John Vincent and Lewis Miller in 1874 to satisfy the "hunger of mind abroad in the land." Despite the jugglers and trained dogs in the more raffish shows, traveling Chautauquas offered glimpses of learning, music, and current events (William Jennings Bryan was an all but permanent fixture) to vast numbers of Americans. The temperance crusade was another frequent small-town visitor; the stern advocate at left poses with a variety of scientific props and a scenic backdrop in Ely, Minnesota.

WESTERN HISTORY COLLECTIONS, UNIVERSITY OF OKLAHOMA LIBRARY

In enterprising towns such as Guthrie in Oklahoma Territory, local talent was utilized to organize theatricals. H. T. Swearingen took this self-captioned picture, but just what the troupe and its child star performed is not explained.

PHOTOGRAPHIC ARCHIVES, UNIVERSITY OF LOUISVILLE

A common form of family "entertainment" was the simple stroll. While buggy rides into the countryside were favored by the town dandies—William Allen White recalled that in his courting days $1.50 would rent a horse and buggy for all Sunday afternoon—there were usually worthwhile destinations within range of shanks' mare. The impressive High Bridge (above) that carried a railroad across the Kentucky River near Wilmore, Kentucky, for example, was worth seeing, and A. B. Rue of Harrodsburg thought it worth photographing. Putt Telfer took the picture opposite along the shore of Otsego Lake near Cooperstown, New York; the strollers surely stopped to commiserate with the gloomy car owner.

OVERLEAF: If it is possible to take a portrait of complete tranquillity, then William L. Bennett succeeded in July of 1896 near Navarre, Ohio, when he made this contemplative view of an old lock on the abandoned Ohio and Erie Canal.

MASSILLON MUSEUM

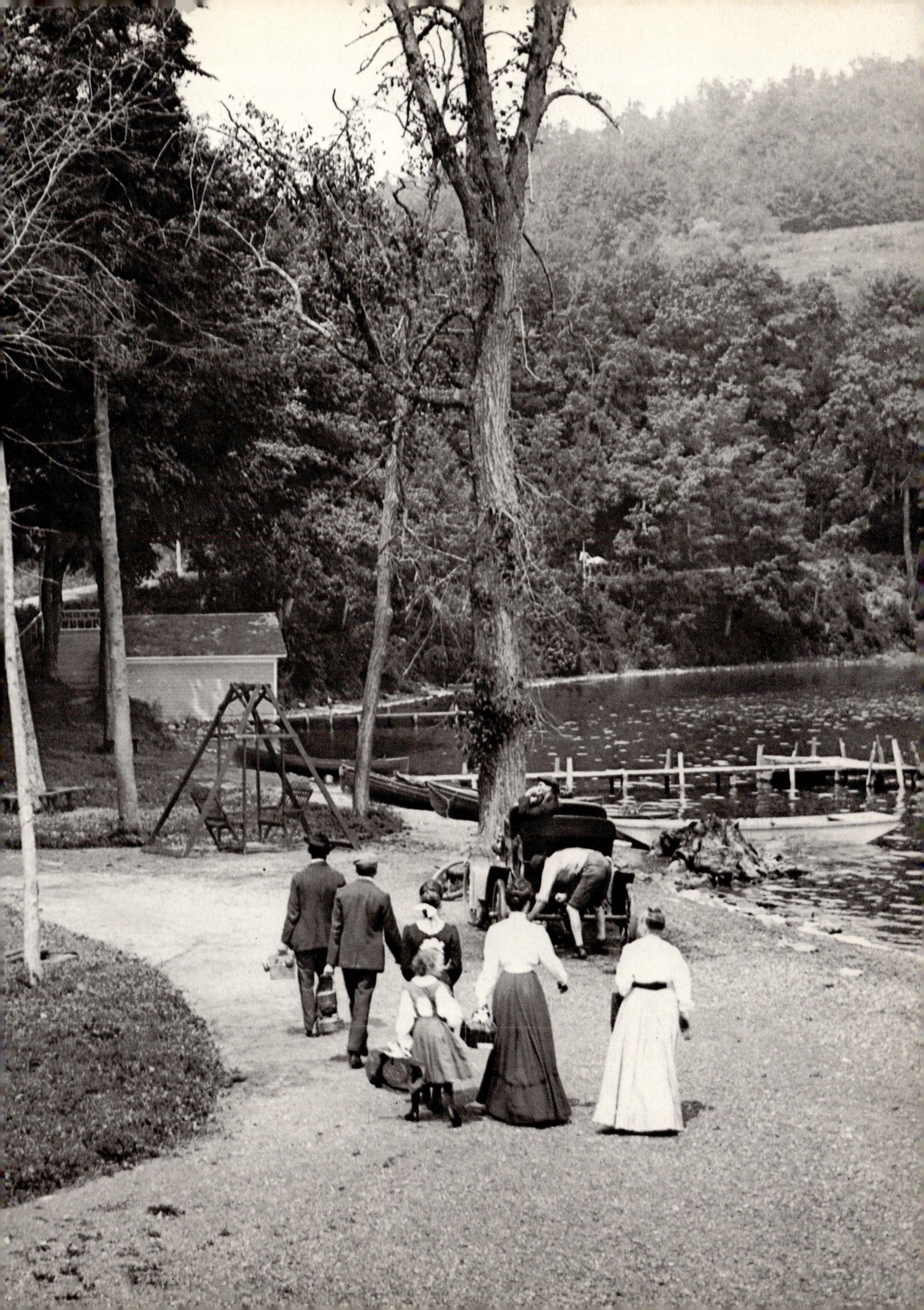

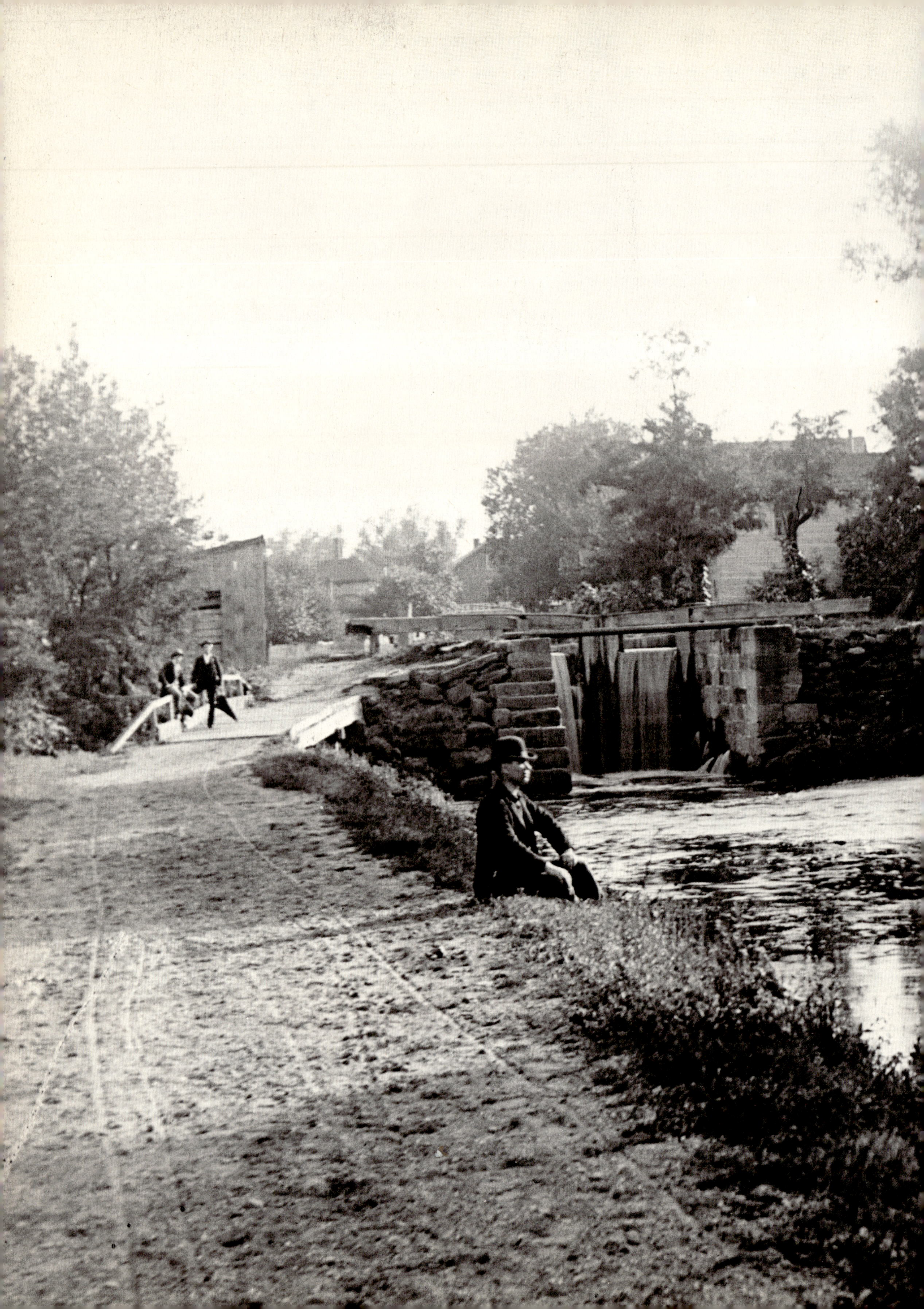

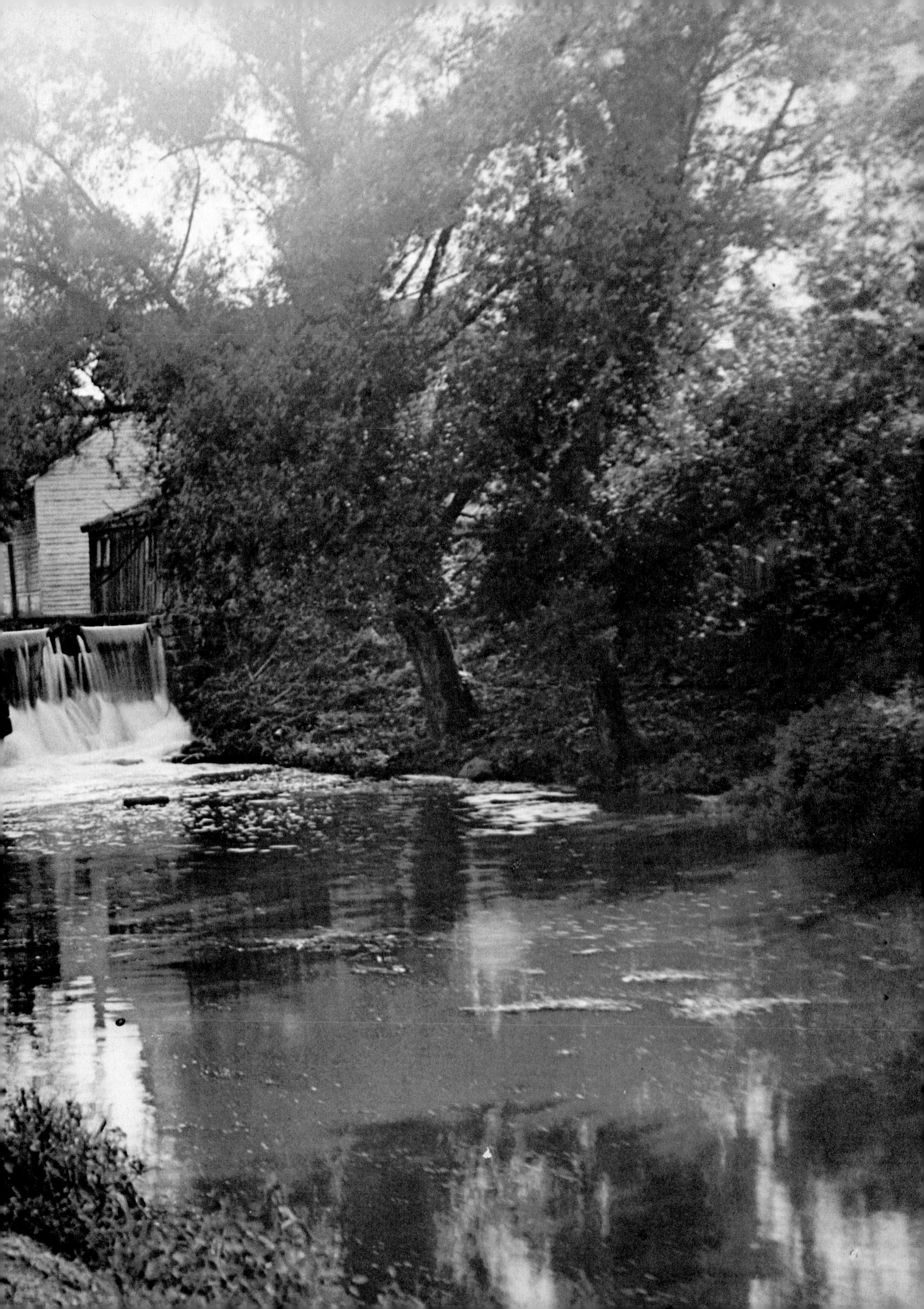

In common with most other small-town amusements, wintertime activities were usually simple in nature and undertaken close to home. Most cold-weather traveling in the northern latitudes was by train, which is presumably the way the Drake family of Corning, New York, reached Keuka Lake to go ice-boating (above). Isabel Drake took the picture in March, 1907. The crowd below, about to make a run aboard a type of bobsled that some called, with vivid directness, a double ripper, was enjoying the pleasures of Saranac Lake, New York, in the 1890's. Mrs. Bernard photographed the bowlegged snowman and his friend.

CULVER PICTURES

Mr. A. B. Rue of Harrodsburg, Kentucky, labeled his view above "Mercer County's famous fishing dam"; the log dam and the relaxed anglers are believed to be on the Salt River. The scene at the right reflects considerably more strenuous activity—not only the pedaling that was required to reach this spot, but the effort that went into hauling all those bicycles into position for the picture-taking. The reason for it all becomes clear upon close inspection of the fishy character at lower left, across whose chest is written, "We Want Good Roads. We Can't Swim all the Time." The photograph is one bicycle club's part in a campaign for better roads that American cyclists, some one million strong, waged in the mid-Nineties when their sport was all the rage. The setting is the Devil's Oven in Ausable Chasm, a scenic gorge in the Adirondacks near Keeseville, New York, that carries the Ausable River toward Lake Champlain.

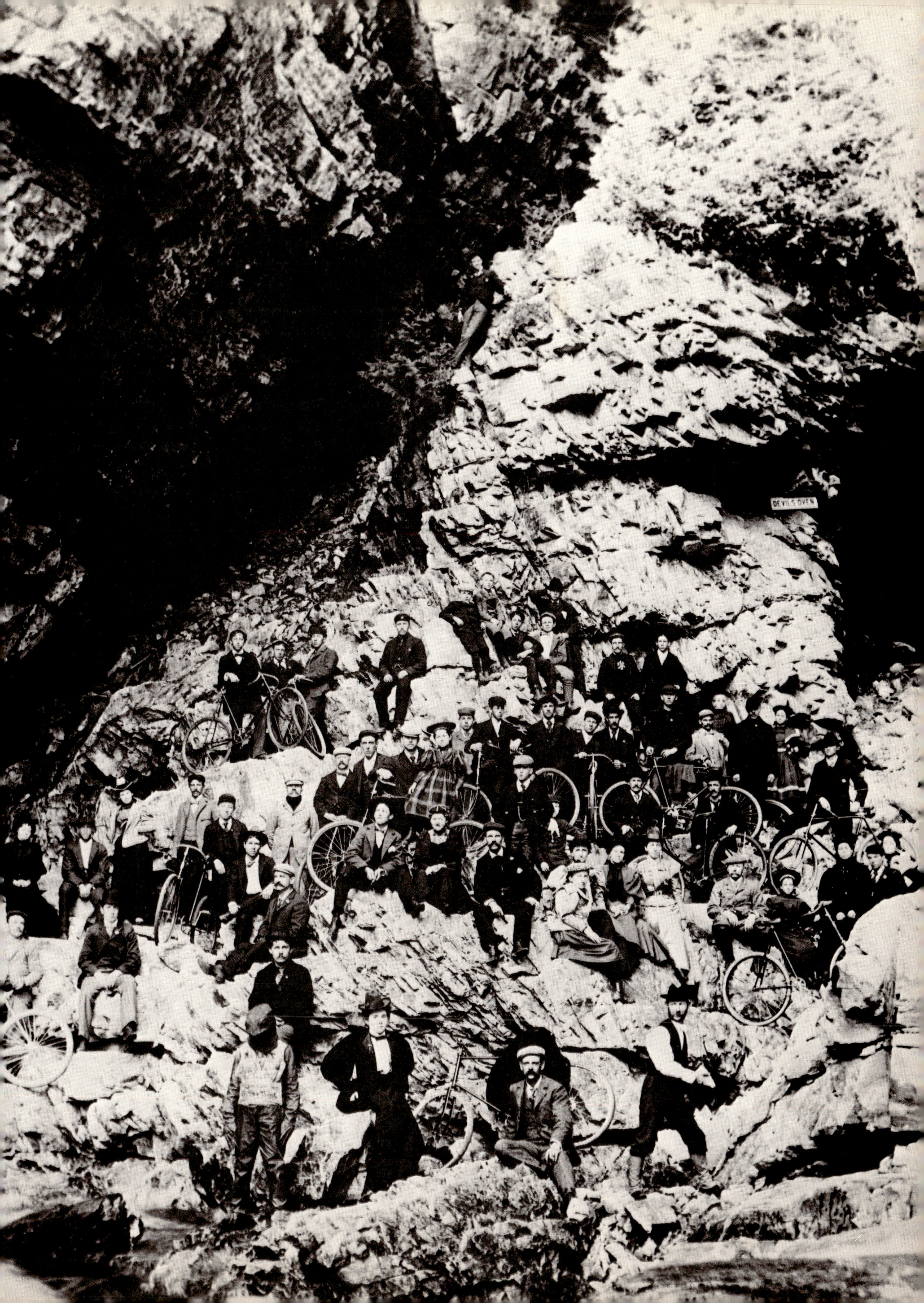
DEVILS OVEN

COLLECTION OF ROBERT L. WEICHERT

The well-established fishing camp opposite was photographed about
1900 by Wills White of Bennington, Vermont. It was located
in Woodford, a village near Bennington popular for hunting, fishing,
and picnicing. Between the pistol-packing young man at the right
and the highly respectable gentleman at the left, the young ladies
were safe from all harm. The bathers below (like the campers, well
chaperoned) testing the waters of Otsego Lake at about the same
date were photographed by Cooperstown's Telfer. Undoubtedly nothing
came of the fear expressed a few years earlier by an editor that
ladies' bathing costumes such as these would inspire "a riot of personal
license between the sexes which leaves nothing to the imagination."

NEW YORK STATE HISTORICAL ASSOCIATION

The Sunday excursionists aboard the narrow-gauge logging train above were from Harbor Springs, a village on Michigan's Little Traverse Bay. Whether the fishermen below were coming or going on Cooperstown's interurban line, they were well prepared. Pictured opposite is an all-day outing aboard the rough-and-ready Missouri River steamer *Nadine,* photographed about 1905 by Dr. Charles Swap of Boonville, Missouri.

MISSOURI HISTORICAL SOCIETY

DETROIT PUBLISHING COMPANY COLLECTION, LIBRARY OF CONGRESS

The summer vacation was not yet an institution in the United States at the turn of the century, but it was growing in popularity among the urban affluent and the small-town upper crust. For some it meant an exclusive retreat such as Cuttyhunk Island (right) off the Massachusetts coast, where avid fishermen could go for striped bass from fishing stands. Eastern nature lovers stormed into the beautiful Adirondacks. The natty hikers photographed above in 1903 were rewarded for a modest 540-foot climb to the summit of Bald Mountain with a fine view of the Fulton Chain Lakes.

WHALING MUSEUM, NEW BEDFORD, MASS.

ALL: AMERICAN HERITAGE COLLECTION

Of all the small-town life styles to be found as the twentieth century began, few could have been more attractive than that of the James Drake family of Corning, New York. In June after school was out, banker Drake—the top man in the leapfrog demonstration at right—bundled his family off to Drake Point on Keuka Lake for the summer. It was a place of cool deep porches and sun-dappled shadows and laughing children splashing along the shoreline. Between the stable and the icehouse a casual family baseball game sprang up periodically, with trees for bases and rustic benches for spectators in straw boaters or middy blouses. A shifting, itinerant population of friends and relatives was also on hand—such as the two young men at left playing pole ball—and the whole cheerful menagerie of people and pets at rest and play was recorded by Mrs. Drake's camera.

STATE HISTORICAL SOCIETY OF WISCONSIN

CHARLES PHELPS CUSHING

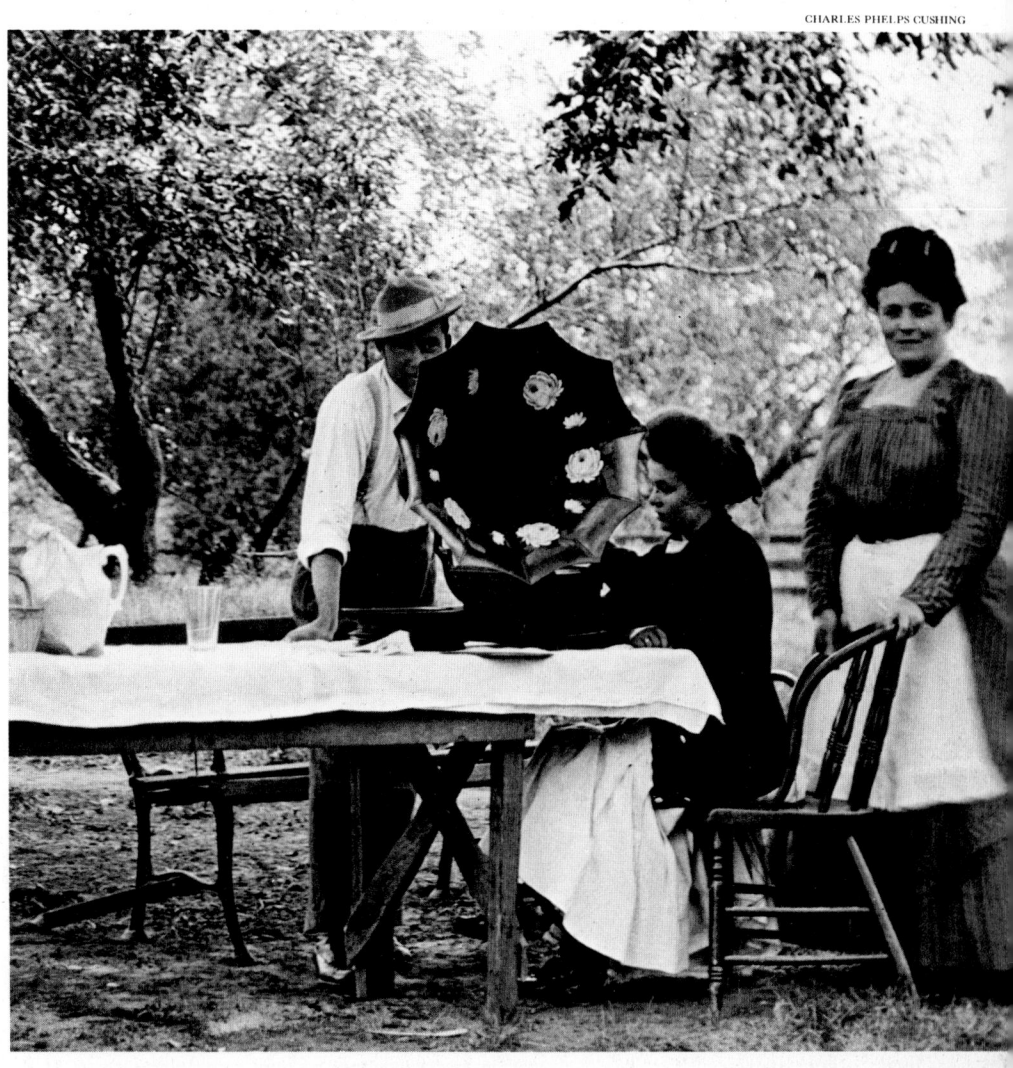

Summertime was picnic time, and a big picnic staged by the town or by fraternal or social groups such as the Masons or the Grange offered a full day's entertainment along with a full stomach. The barbeque at left was a community effort by the citizens of Menomonie, Wisconsin, who in 1899 hired an expert, one "Mr. Wilson of Indiana," to marshal the resources needed to turn out thirteen quarters of beef and 8,000 pints of burgoo. Mr. Wilson's operation, at the local trotting track, was thought to be worth watching. The vignette above was photographed at a Grange picnic in Olathe, Kansas, about 1910. It is possible to imagine the scratchy melodies blaring forth from the flower horn: a quartet harmonizing "The Old Oaken Bucket," or perhaps a tenor warbling away at "Hello, Central! Give Me Heaven."

MASSILLON MUSEUM

When these pictures were taken, Civil War veterans' organizations were much in evidence across the country, demonstrating a talent for political clout and an interest in social activities. At left are veterans of the 104th Ohio infantry regiment and their families posing for an annual reunion picture on the porch of the pavilion at Meyer's Lake in the 1880's. The regiment, raised in and around Massillon, chipped in to have a portrait painted of its beloved fox terrier mascot, who had trotted alongside the boys when they marched through Georgia with Sherman. For celebrity, however, no Civil War mascot could touch Old Abe the battle eagle, pride and joy of the 8th Wisconsin. Old Abe reputedly saw some combat, picturesquely flapping his wings and screaming defiance at the Johnny Rebs, and after the war he enjoyed an honored retirement in the basement of the state capital in Madison. In 1881 he expired in a fire, but after the ministrations of a taxidermist his spirit went marching on. In Van Schaick's photograph below, Old Abe heads a parade of the Women's Relief Corps (an auxiliary of the Grand Army of the Republic) in Black River Falls in 1890.

STATE HISTORICAL SOCIETY OF WISCONSIN

COLLECTION OF RON RYDER

At the turn of the century harness racing was the single most popular spectator sport in small-town America. Here is a tense moment at the county fairgrounds track at Boonville, New York. The grandstand is at left, the race officials' perch and bandstand at right, and every eye is on the tight contest. "The crowd in the grand-stand rose to their feet as the field of trotters came down the homestretch," wrote Herbert Quick, an Iowa lawyer and author, of what must have been a strikingly similar scene. "The marshals yelled at the track-side throng to keep back . . . and when they came to the wire, with the sorrel still taking the pole, the black leading him by a neck, the roan and bay hurling themselves forward . . . you should have heard the roar which arose from that Iowa crowd."

BOTH: PHOTOGRAPHIC ARCHIVES, UNIVERSITY OF LOUISVILLE

Harness races no doubt helped the draw at county fairs, but a primary attraction remained the agricultural exhibits. On the opposite page are prize-winning Kentuckians about the time of World War I. The four young ladies most likely raised their blue-ribbon heifers themselves, but the young man below them was only in the picture for his photogenic qualities; he gets some help handling his impressive charge from offstage right. The gentleman above is Mr. Barckly Southerland of Carlsbad, New Mexico Territory, who was in charge of an exhibit of the best produce raised by Carlsbad's 1,700 or so citizens at a fair in the metropolis of Albuquerque (population *c.* 11,000) in 1908. Carlsbad's best appears impressive indeed, especially as displayed in those fancy outsized canning jars.

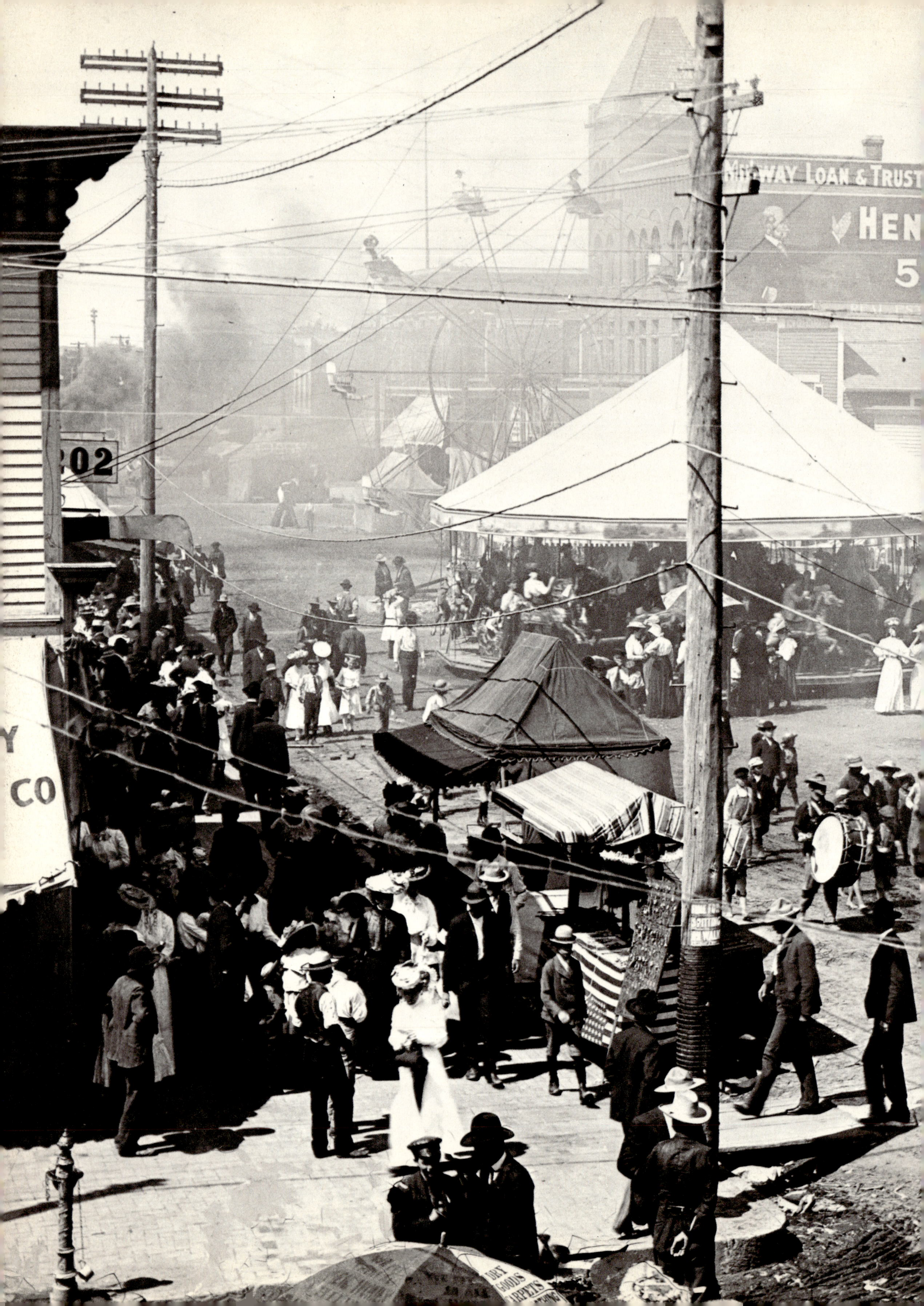

MIDWAY LOAN & TRUST
HEN
5
202
CO

There were growing complaints from small-town preachers and editors about the midway tent shows that infiltrated county fairs toward the end of the century. A Wisconsin official charged that "gaudy shows, gambling devices, organ-grinding, conjuring, mountebankism, and every species of graceless vagabondism" were becoming commonplace at fairs, and an Iowa editor dismissed midway proprietors as "blacklegs and swindlers." He no doubt meant types such as the county-fair barker and snake handler above, shilling for Larry the Cigarette Fiend. The traveling carnival at left, set up squarely in the middle of Kearney, Nebraska, was photographed by Solomon Butcher in 1907. It is a medley of rich impressions: the tootling bandsmen, the whirling merry-go-round, the slowly turning ferris wheel; at center is a souvenir stand and at right under the canopy are peep-show machines to titillate the farm boys. In Kearney in 1907 the Gibson girl look was in, everyone wore a hat, and a carnival drew a crowd.

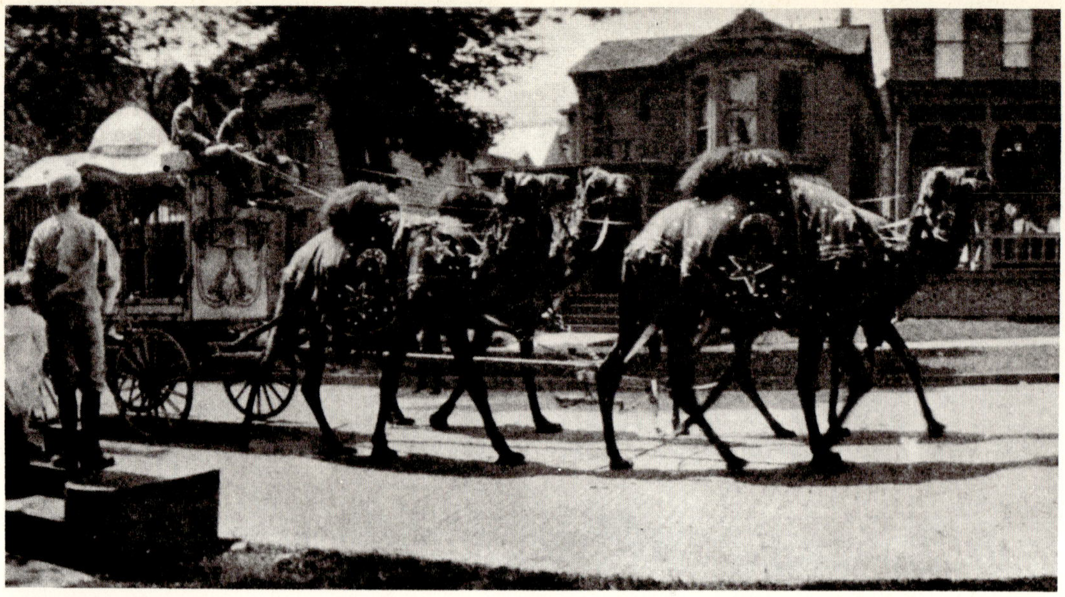

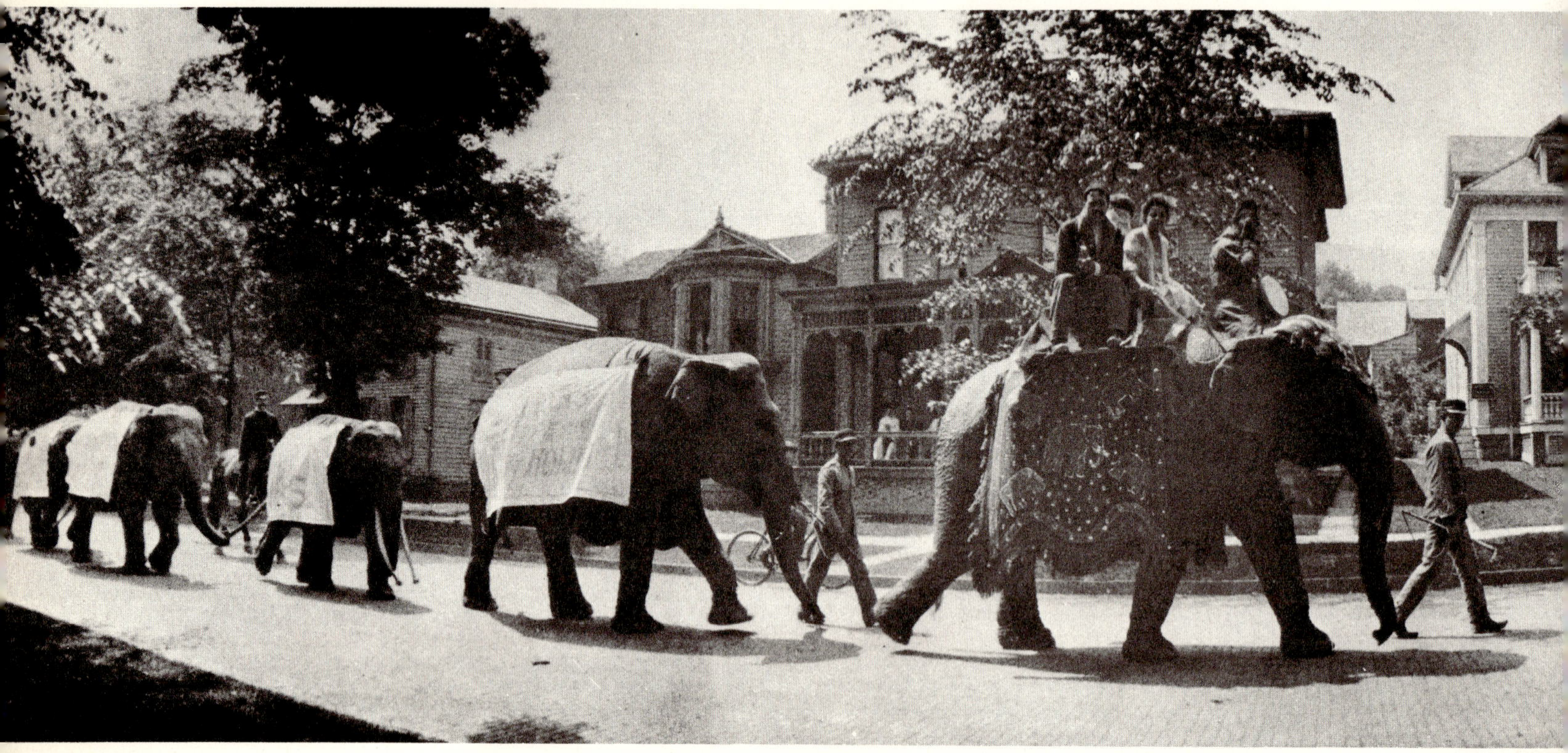

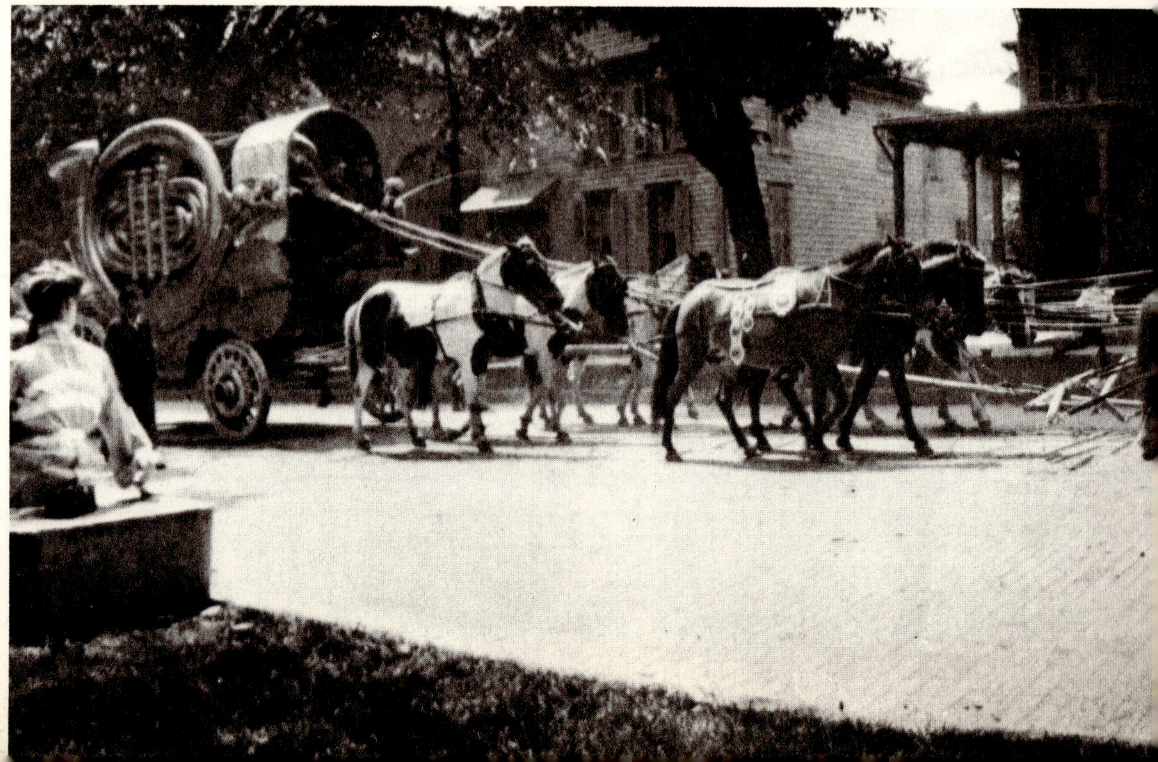

It is June, 1904, and Isabel Drake has positioned herself with her Kodak panoramic camera on a front lawn on First Street in Corning, New York, to record the gaudy passage of the Robinson circus. "The parade was paramount, the performance a matter of indifference," wrote Gerard E. Jensen of his youth in Norwich, Connecticut. "We had viewed the real drama of circus life, we had taken in a free show of the first quality, and all else was of no consequence. When we had seen the parade we had seen all." Jensen's view of the comparative merits of parade and performance might get an argument, but there is no disputing the fact that the circus was regarded as a major entertainment event of the year.

ALL: AMERICAN HERITAGE COLLECTION

MASSILLON MUSEUM

HARRY RANSOM HUMANITIES RESEARCH CENTER, UNIVERSITY OF TEXAS AT AUSTIN

"The local band outranked all other musical organizations in popularity," writes Lewis Atherton. It was called upon every Decoration Day, Fourth of July, and Founder's Day, livened up special excursions, and accompanied visiting artists at the opera house. And there were the afternoon or evening band concerts so vivid in memoirists' recollections. "I can recall now, after seventy years, hearing the Eldorado silver cornet band playing down in Burdette's grove by the mill," wrote William Allen White in his *Autobiography*; it was, he insisted, "heavenly music." The aggregation at upper left, photographed by Theodore Teeple in the Nineties, was the pride and joy of Canal Fulton, Ohio. Below it is the Llano, Texas, cornet band, photographed by W. D. Smithers as it spiced up opening-day ceremonies at a 1907 county fair. Both Canal Fulton and Llano had populations of between 1,000 and 2,000, but even the hamlet of White Pine, Colorado, with fewer than a hundred residents, had a brass group, taken (above) by Frank Dean in 1890.

No holiday exceeded the Fourth of July for sheer entertainment value. The leading community groups—volunteer firemen, ladies' auxiliaries, fraternal lodges, old soldiers—got together to present a day's program that might range from sack races to a balloon ascension. The daring gentleman above is Mr. Dorr Derby of Williamsville, Vermont, doing the warm-up for his annual Fourth of July spectacular—a headstand atop the local basket factory's 70-foot smokestack; Porter Thayer took his picture in 1912. Fishing for "treasure" (below) was one of the day's typical pastimes. The waggish float opposite was the creation of the Fusileers, a group of mummers in Mt. Vision, New York. Putt Telfer of nearby Cooperstown made the photograph in 1911.

OVERLEAF: An unknown photographer captured the essence of a small-town Glorious Fourth, here celebrated on a Vermont village green in the first decade of the century. An orator holds forth from a shadowed speaker's stand (right) hailing the Founding Fathers, extolling the Boys in Blue inscribed on the G.A.R. monument, and closing with a recitation of the Declaration of Independence. No doubt the inattentive shared Bruce Catton's "extremely moderate" boyhood appetite for such orations, yet few would have questioned the spirited confidence and patriotism underlying that day.
CULVER PICTURES

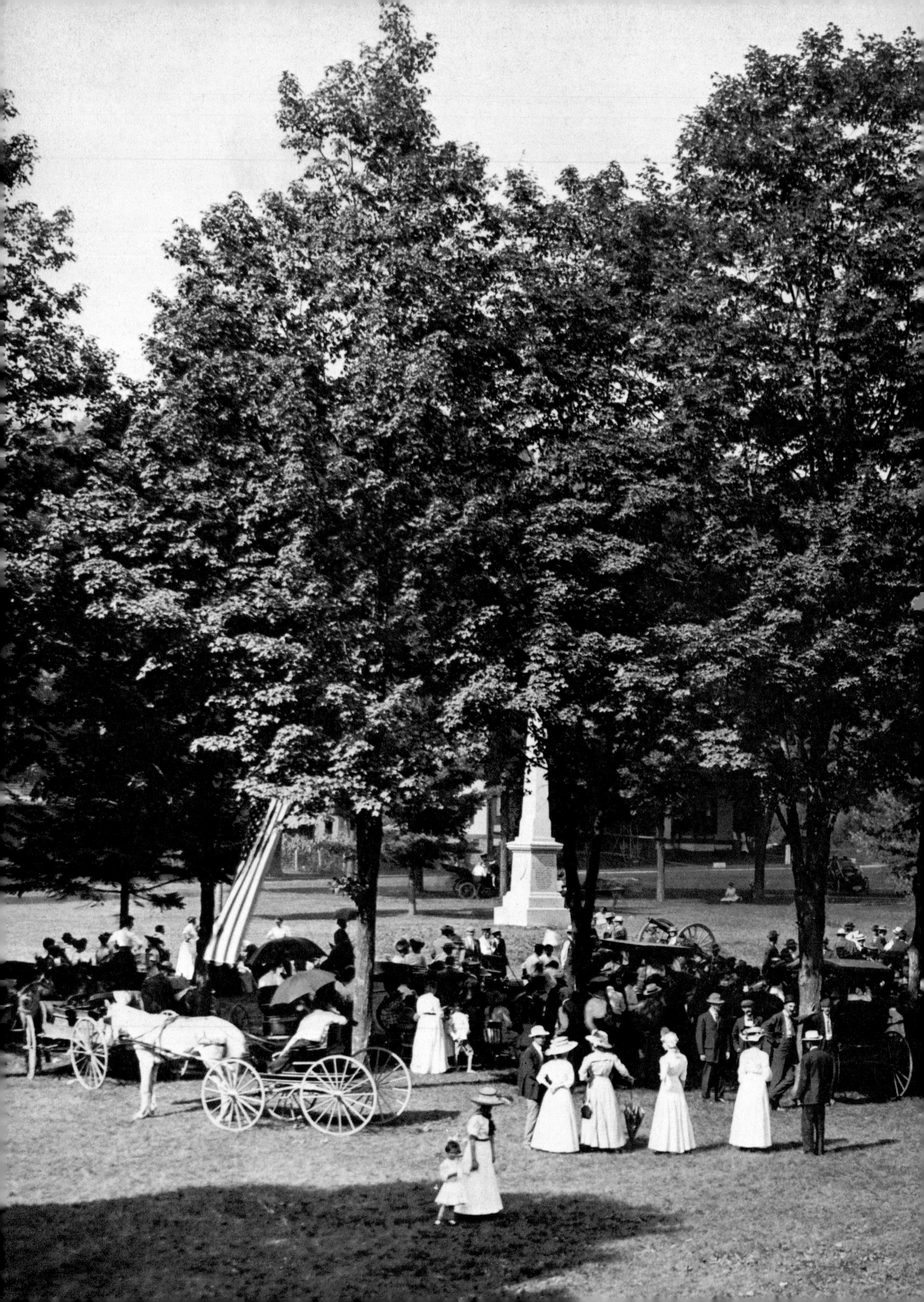

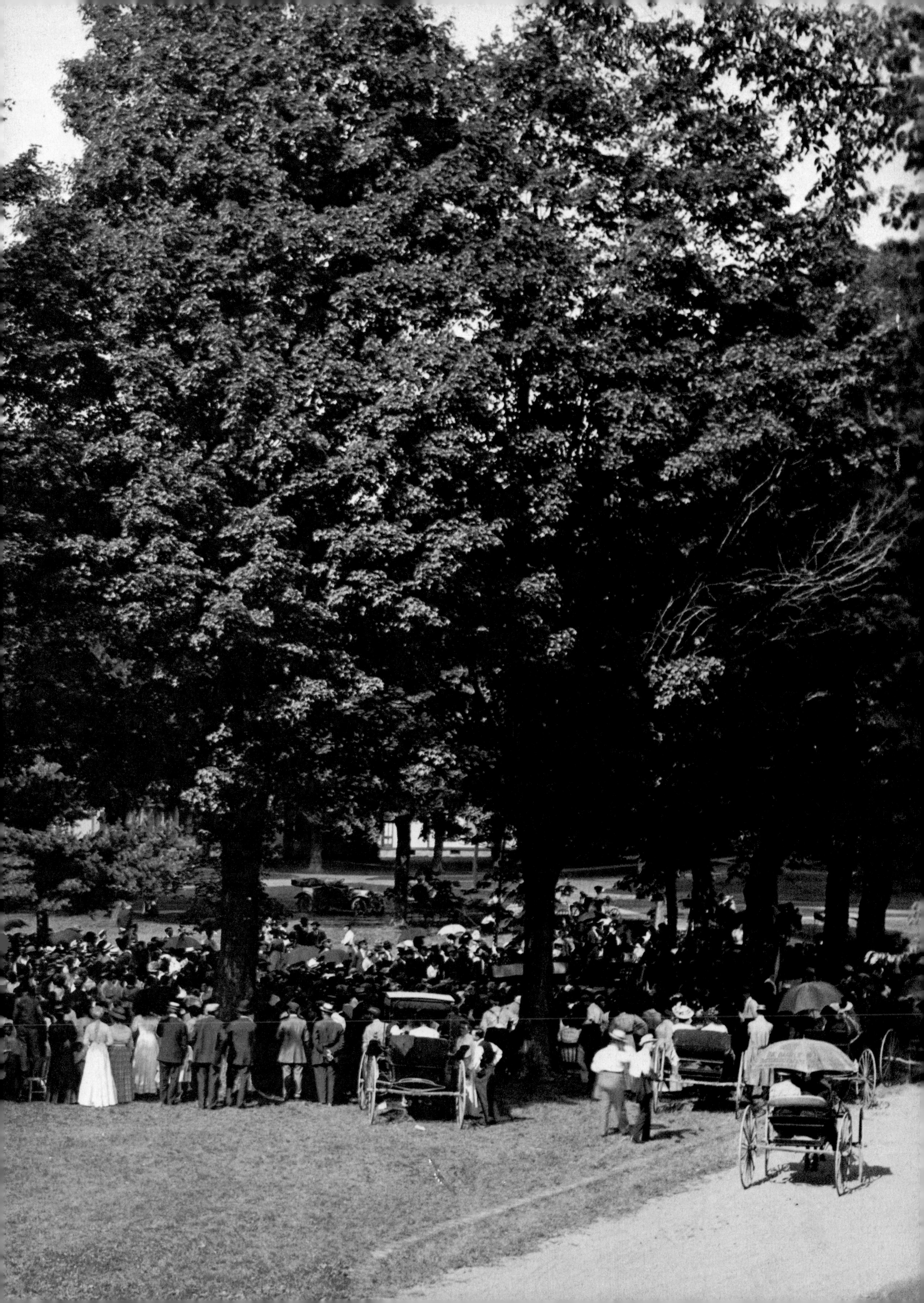

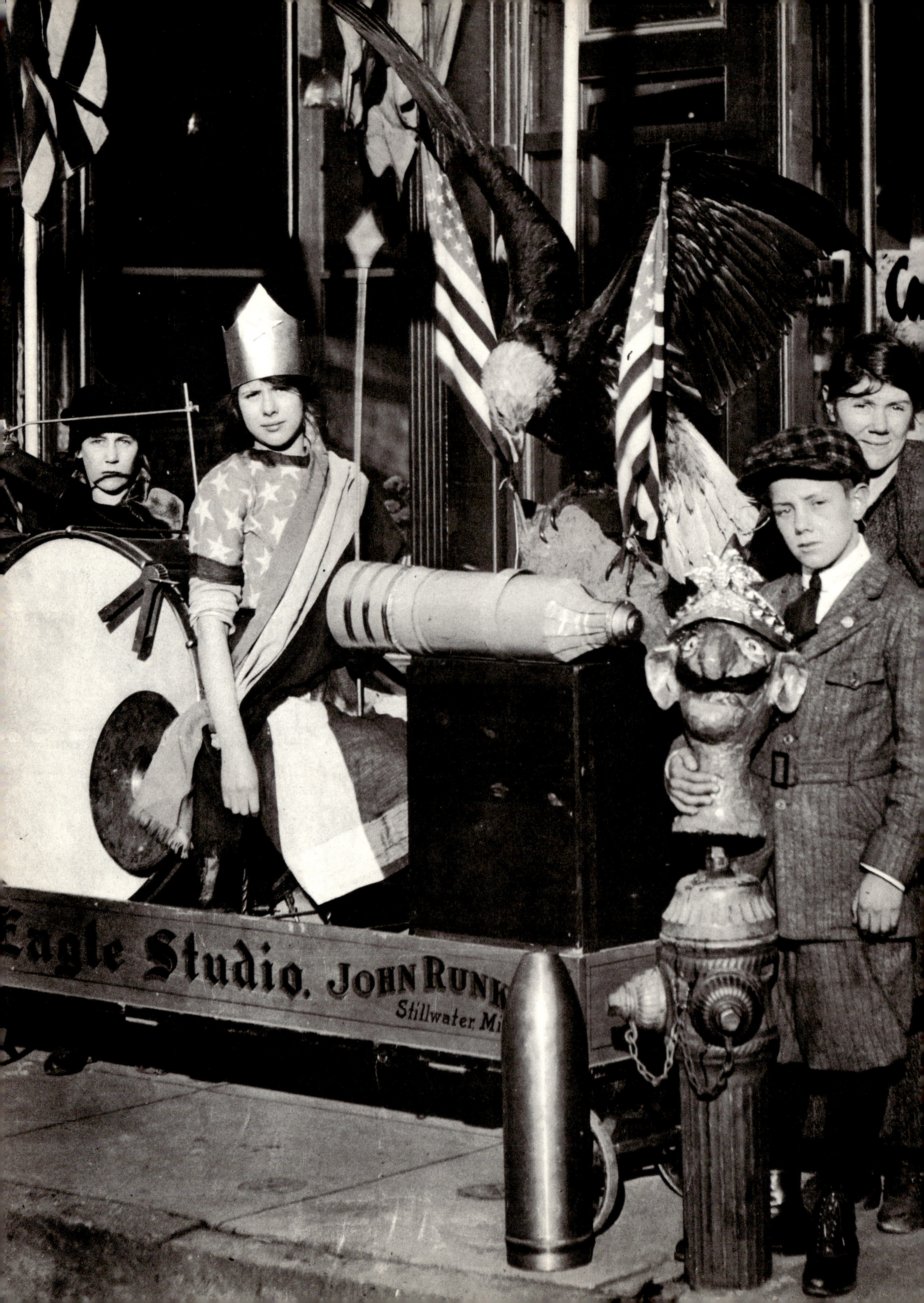
Eagle Studio. JOHN RUNK
Stillwater, Mi

CHAPTER

6

Remembered Moments

Early in November, 1918, the news from the Western Front left little doubt that the war to end wars was nearly done. In Stillwater, Minnesota, photographer John Runk cobbled together a float for the victory celebration he anticipated, and when the Armistice was announced he inserted the date on his banner and hauled the float out in front of his South Main Street studio and took this picture. Miss Columbia was assigned to beat the drum and ting-a-ling the triangle and make other joyous noises. Kaiser Bill's head clutched by the young man in the plaid cap would, when the celebration started, be dangled at the cannon's mouth. The finishing touch, the screaming eagle, was a prop from Runk's American Eagle Studio. The whole antic contraption was perfectly appropriate for that first Armistice Day, one of the last occasions on which twentieth-century Americans publicly displayed an innocent faith in the imminent return of the old days and the old ways.

The family album atop the parlor piano customarily included a selection of such pictures depicting major happenings on the local scene—the first trolley in town, the great flood of '92, the goings-on after Admiral Dewey whipped the Spaniards, the day William Jennings Bryan declaimed from the courthouse steps. These were the special events that interrupted the daily routine, and what follows is a sampling from archives and family albums across the nation.

Whether treasured or regretted, these were moments that engraved themselves in the memory. Take, for example, this recollection by Mississippian Murry Falkner, brother of the famous novelist (who spelled the family name his own way): "The great day had finally come, the one on which a man was going aloft in a real balloon," Falkner wrote, "and surely nobody was more keyed up with anticipation and wonder than Bill and John and myself." The balloon turned out to be tattered and lumpy and its pilot a surly lout awash in whiskey, but on that day in 1907 nothing could have dragged the three Falkner brothers away from the preparations in Oxford's town square. When the balloon soared aloft the boys were ecstatic—it was drifting straight toward their house on the edge of town. Cross-lots they raced, tripping and scrambling as they tried to keep the craft in sight. Finally they tumbled into their back lot, face to face with their wrathful mother and "covered with soot, with clothes ripped and torn, and with gashes all over us. But it couldn't be helped: we had lived with this splendid aircraft too long to give it up before the end—which was fast approaching. There was a quick and heavy swish . . . as the collapsed bag enveloped the barn and the basket plunked down onto the roof of the chicken house. It dumped the pilot out onto the roof on the back of his neck; his hand holding the crock made a big arc, smashing into the shingles and breaking the crock, from which whiskey poured down on the unsuspecting chickens calmly at roost below. Instantly they set up a cackling that could be heard a mile away." It was a magnificent spectacle, one the Falkner boys considered well worth the fearful scolding about to descend on them.

Henry Seidel Canby, it will be recalled, positioned turn-of-the-century Americans in an Age of Confidence. Perhaps the clearest manifestation of this confidence was their unblinking faith in Progress—a term given the weight and substance of Newtonian law. According to Lewis Mumford, Progress may be defined as man's success in imposing "his own machine-conditioned fantasies upon nature"; thanks to "daring inventors and even more daring prophets," he continues, "this period was destined, almost everyone then confidently supposed, to produce even greater wonders than the steam engine, the electric telegraph, the Hoe printing press, the dynamo. . . ."

There was, for example, the transportation revolution that marched into small-town America in this period. Horsecars and trolleys and interurban lines began shredding the isolation that had encased towns from the days of their founding. The horsecars and the trolleys promoted economic growth and were welcomed with the enthusiasm demonstrated by the Californians on pages 196-197, and the interurban opened up whole new vistas of travel.

The revolution gathered momentum with the arrival of the motorcar. No doubt the good people of Pasadena greeted the first one to chug into town with the same delight they had showered on the first horsecar. Early in the century autos were relatively rare, quite expensive, and frequently unreliable. That soon changed. By 1911 Mr. Ford's industrial juggernaut was starting to roll as he doubled production of the Model T (to 34,500 units) and pared its price by $170 (to $780), and in the century's second decade the automobile initiated changes in the small-town landscape that proved irrevocable. In those ten years the nation's motor vehicle population multplied twenty times, to over 9.2 million, all but ending the isolation of the country town. Suddenly, writes Lewis Atherton, "Main Street had to learn to compete with the outside world."

In *Williamstown Branch*, his memoir of growing up in a Vermont village, R. L. Duffus remarks on the appetites of "the Thing with wheels but no horse": "The Thing killed Williamstown, and not out of cussedness, but because it was so demanding. The Thing demanded a different kind of road from the one on which Cousin Joanna and I went [buggy] riding. . . . The Thing had no thought of a road taken at leisure, tasted and relished; the Thing had to be somewhere at a given time, anyhow in a great hurry; the Thing wished to hustle and dash, not stroll." Once the town had been like an island, producing for itself most of life's necessities, Duffus explained. "Williamstown could do this, no matter what it took in from the outside world. It didn't make all its own flour, but it could have; nor process all its own meat, but it could have; nor raise all its own vegetables, but it could have. . . . Williamstown people could have stayed alive for a long while if the Central Vermont Railway had stopped running and the dirt roads had been blocked." That did not happen: Progress does not allow for backsliding.

The economic shift from local self-sufficiency and independence to interdependence—that spin-off of the industrial revolution begun decades before and transported to the site by rail—was speeded up rapidly by the flivver and the motor truck. As an ever-growing percentage of the nation's work force was employed in industry, small-towners started commuting to the factories by automobile or pulling up stakes in favor of city living. Almost overnight there were too many market towns; the number needed to serve the farmer in the age of the horse showed a surplus in the age of the wide-ranging Model T. Often local industries could not meet the competition of bigger trade centers, and truck-supplied chain stores became a threat to Main Street's merchants. In short, economic interdependency meant that small towns increasingly imported their goods and services from the outside world and exported labor and whatever else might still be profitably produced locally. Places whose resulting "balance of trade" was negative began to fade; those that through adaptation or good fortune achieved a favorable balance survived.

How Progress operated (and still operates) was summarized by reporter Andrew H. Malcolm in a 1974 dispatch to the New York *Times* relating the closing of the Hoag turkey feather duster factory in Monticello, Iowa. Handsome, utilitarian Hoag dusters were equal to the ultimate in housekeeping challenges—Victorian parlor bric-a-brac—but after 102 years they had fallen victim to Progress in the form of aerosol sprays and polishes. It was the climax to decades of Progress in Monticello, reported Malcolm: "The Ma and Pa grocery store is bought out by A & P. Phyllis's Feminine Fashions goes out of business, an economic sacrifice to the department store in the sprawling shopping center by the growing city that was once a two-day ride away. Now it is just 30 power-steered minutes down a paved highway. Then one day the townspeople realize it has been years since anyone parked a tractor on Main Street. And most of the men and women earn a living in a factory in some metal prefab building near the old railroad depot, which is now a boutique."

The new competition with the outside world involved more than economics. The small-town's social and cultural milieu, exposed for the first time to relatively sophisticated urban standards, was apt to wilt in the spotlight. The simple, innocent pleasures of a Sunday afternoon, the earnest amateur theatricals at the opera house, suddenly appeared hopelessly old-fashioned and bumpkinish. The new motion pictures (pages 200-201), crude and flickering as they might be, seemed far more worldly and exciting than a medicine show or a hose-company competition. The gulf between the two worlds widened as many of the best and brightest small-towners were drawn to the city's lights and opportunities, taking with them the imagination that had energized whatever intellectual climate was to be found within the town limits.

Consequently—although not due to any inherent, fatal flaw in its make-up—the small town's comfortable, self-confident, self-contained way of life, long nourished in isolation from the world at large, was rapidly overwhelmed by Progress. Not surprisingly, Progress turned out to be neither an unvarnished curse nor an unmixed blessing. It ended many of the old, pleasant ways forever, yet it succeeded in easing some of the heaviest burdens of daily living. New job opportunities, new intellectual challenges, and new sights to see broadened the horizons of many.

Canby is quoted in an earlier chapter making the point that life as we experience it flourishes when it marches to a steady rhythm but is "upset by its changes, weakened by its loss." American society as a whole was subjected to radical changes of rhythm beginning about the time of the First World War. "A new era was beginning," Bruce Catton writes. "No one was prepared, anywhere, and the deeper we get into this new era the more baffling it becomes. All that seems clear is that the mind of man now is obliged to adjust itself (without loss of time, and under penalty of death) to the greatest revolution in human history; a revolution, not in the relations of class with class and society with society, but in the nature of man's idea of the universe and of his place in it. . . . We can go anywhere and do anything, and because the fabulous machine we have created can neither be reversed, put in neutral or turned aside we have to go and do to the utmost limit. . . ." Small-town America, already experiencing the complications of "emerging-nation" status, was strongly affected by this fluctuation of rhythm. Most small-towners, indeed most small towns, survived the upheaval, but the changes that resulted—economic, social, psychological—were permanent.

Whatever the future might bring, that first glimpse of Progress was often a moment to remember. In *The Good Old Days* David L. Cohn recalls the hot summer afternoon early in the century in his hometown of Greenville, Mississippi, when he saw his first horseless carriage. One moment he was hosing down the dusty road in front of the house; the next, Greenville's "pioneer automobilist," Mr. Leroy Wall, "comes thundering across my horizon at twelve miles an hour. Will Butler, the Negro blacksmith in the shop across the way, drops the hoof of the mule he is shoeing and runs to the door to see this latest and most terrifying example of white folks' madness. . . . A flock of chickens, dust-bathing in the road, flies squawking in panic; a two-mule team, bringing a load of firewood to town, skitters into a ditch; while I retreat for safety behind the big cottonwoods that line the sidewalk and, with thumping heart, watch Leroy Wall disappear in a cloud of dust and glory."

HISTORICAL COLLECTIONS, SECURITY PACIFIC NATIONAL BANK

196

It was a great day in Pasadena, California, in 1886 as the Pasadena Street Railroad opened for business, initiating horsecar service (actually mule-powered) from Orange Grove Avenue to Raymond Station, thence to Colorado Street. A gala for fifty invited guests included a trip over the route and dinner here at the Grand Hotel. Waving the flag is Mr. G. Roscoe Thomas.

Beginning in the Nineties, the interurban provided popular short-haul passenger service throughout the nation, particularly between smaller communities that lacked rail connections. Putt Telfer of Cooperstown, something of an interurban buff, was official photographer for a local line, the Oneonta, Cooperstown & Richfield Springs, and he took these pictures around 1900. The phases of construction shown above include hacking out a roadbed cut, installing rail, stringing wire from a makeshift tower car, and laying track on Main Street in Cooperstown—all performed with a minimum of machinery and a maximum of manpower. The splendid parlor car at right was the pride of the O.C. & R.S. and a far cry from the more typical interurban scene wittily caricatured in Fontaine Fox's "Toonerville Trolley" cartoons. Travel aboard the electric cars was exhilarating, "an experience virtually impossible to duplicate today," claims interurban authority William D. Middleton. The automobile did them in.

OVERLEAF: By 1915 in country towns across the land, writes Lewis Atherton, "movies were rapidly destroying the old opera-house regime." Here is the Temple Theatre in Canandaigua, New York, a onetime church now offering the "cleanest show in town" for a nickel; Floyd Gunnison photographed a musical promotion for the current attraction about 1913. This particular "sensational 4-part feature" was described by a critic (already movie critics were jaded, sneering) as the "familiar husband-lost-in-the-war, old homestead mortgaged, stolen will variety" of melodrama. (Following amnesia, frame-ups, and assorted mayhem, the husband was restored to the arms of his faithful Girl of the Sunny South.) One of the coming attractions was Pearl White in "The Heart of an Artist."

INTERNATIONAL MUSEUM OF PHOTOGRAPHY, GEORGE EASTMAN HOUSE

ATRE
Coming "FRIDAY"
CRYSTAL-UNIVERSAL
THE HEART OF AN ARTIST
PEARL WHITE
Coming THURSDAY
GOLD-SEAL-UNIVERSAL
THE GIRL OF THE SUNNY SOUTH
TO-DAY
THE GIRL OF THE SUNNY SOUTH
"THE GIRL OF THE SUNNY SOUTH."

AMERICAN HERITAGE COLLECTION

BROWN BROTHERS

With the arrival of the motorcar in the first decade of the century, the traditional Sunday stroll or Sunday buggy ride gave way to the Sunday drive. At the top of the facing page is Isabel Drake's picture of the family Cadillac, taken about 1907 in Corning, New York, outside the old carriage house now converted to a garage. The procession of vehicles crossing the railroad tracks, headed by two Model T's, was photographed in the First World War period and certainly looks like a Sunday excursion. But there could be problems, and on this page is a sampling—cranking a waterlogged 1909 Packard; a Model T axle-deep in a country road about 1915; fixing a flat on a Jackson somewhere in the wilds of New Jersey in 1909; and (below) a meeting with old Dobbin in 1907.

MOTOR VEHICLE MANUFACTURERS ASSOCIATION

204

The fast-paced modern age, it seemed, belonged to the bold, and there were many willing to tackle new challenges—for example, automobile touring. On the opposite page a Thomas is piloted along a Southern road about 1910 before an appreciative, well-turned-out audience. The picture may be a set-up shot, possibly a promotion for auto travel, but nevertheless countless small-towners such as these got their first look at a horseless carriage when Glidden Tourers roared by in a cloud of dust. As exciting as the auto age might seem, it was nothing compared to the dawning air age. Below is one of the bold ones, aeronaut Roy Knabenshue, who doffed his coat but not his stiff collar in preparation for some strenuous rowing of his airship. The date is January, 1910, the scene Dominguez Field near the village of Compton, California, site of the first major American air meet.

OVERLEAF: Not until 1910 or so, more than a half-dozen years after the Wright brothers first flew, was heavier-than-air flight widely enough seen (as at Dominguez Field) to be believed. Meanwhile, tangible proof of the air age was furnished by the hot-air balloon. In 1903 Solomon Butcher photographed preparations for an ascension at the fairgrounds in Broken Bow, Nebraska.

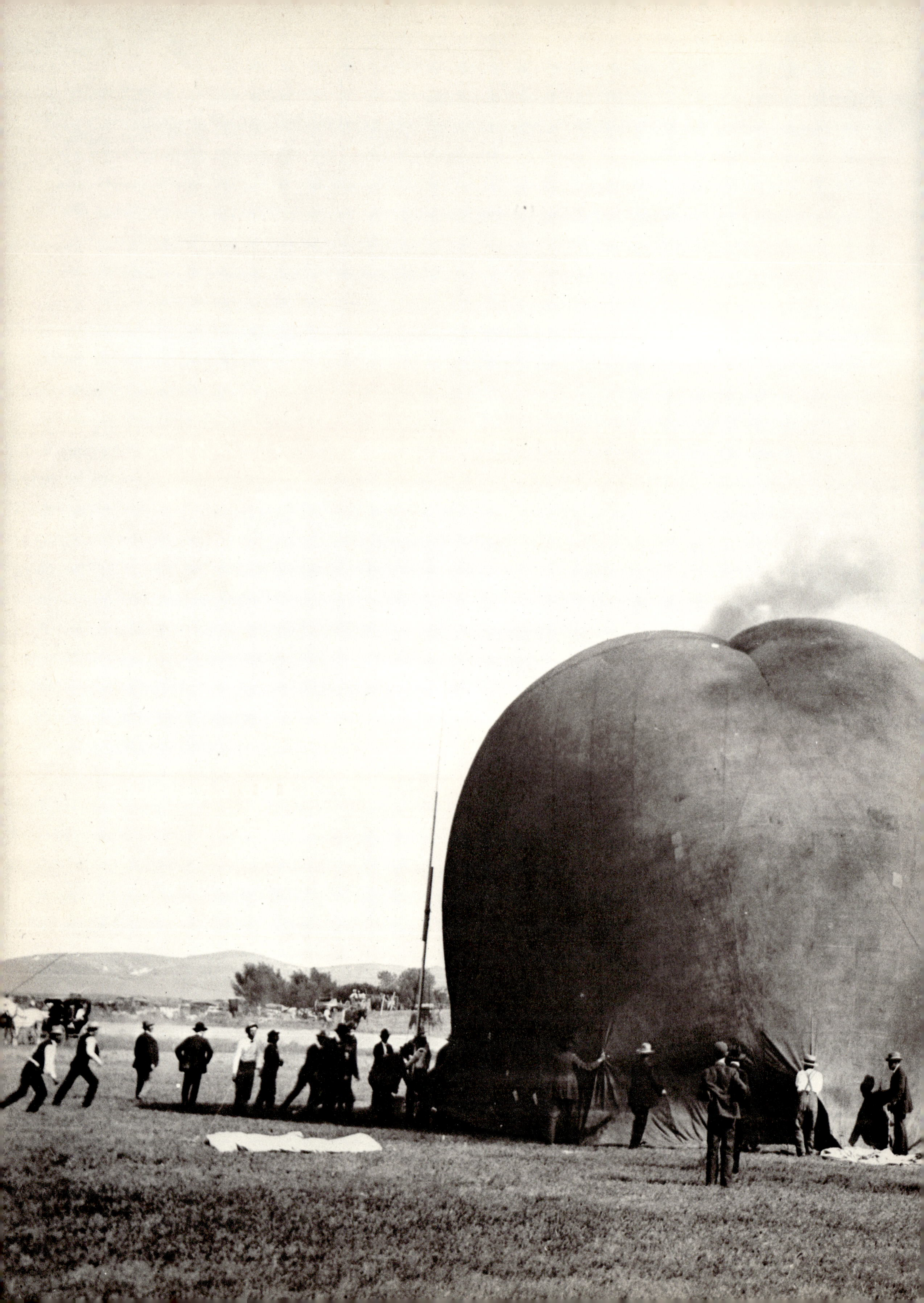

Fires big and small were natural subjects for photographers. A blaze in a furniture store in Roanoke, Virginia, in the mid-Nineties, for instance, caught the eye of scientist and amateur photographer Horace Engle, and the picture at right, taken with his circular-image Kodak, was the result. Cooperstown's Putt Telfer took the view at top of a spectacular conflagration at the local planing mill in 1911. A fire whipped out of control by high winds almost spelled the end for the village of Green Springs, Ohio, in 1908. Before the local volunteer company finally gained the upper hand, seventeen homes and businesses were gutted. As pictured above, Main Street was littered with merchandise and furnishings salvaged by good samaritans from burning stores.

208

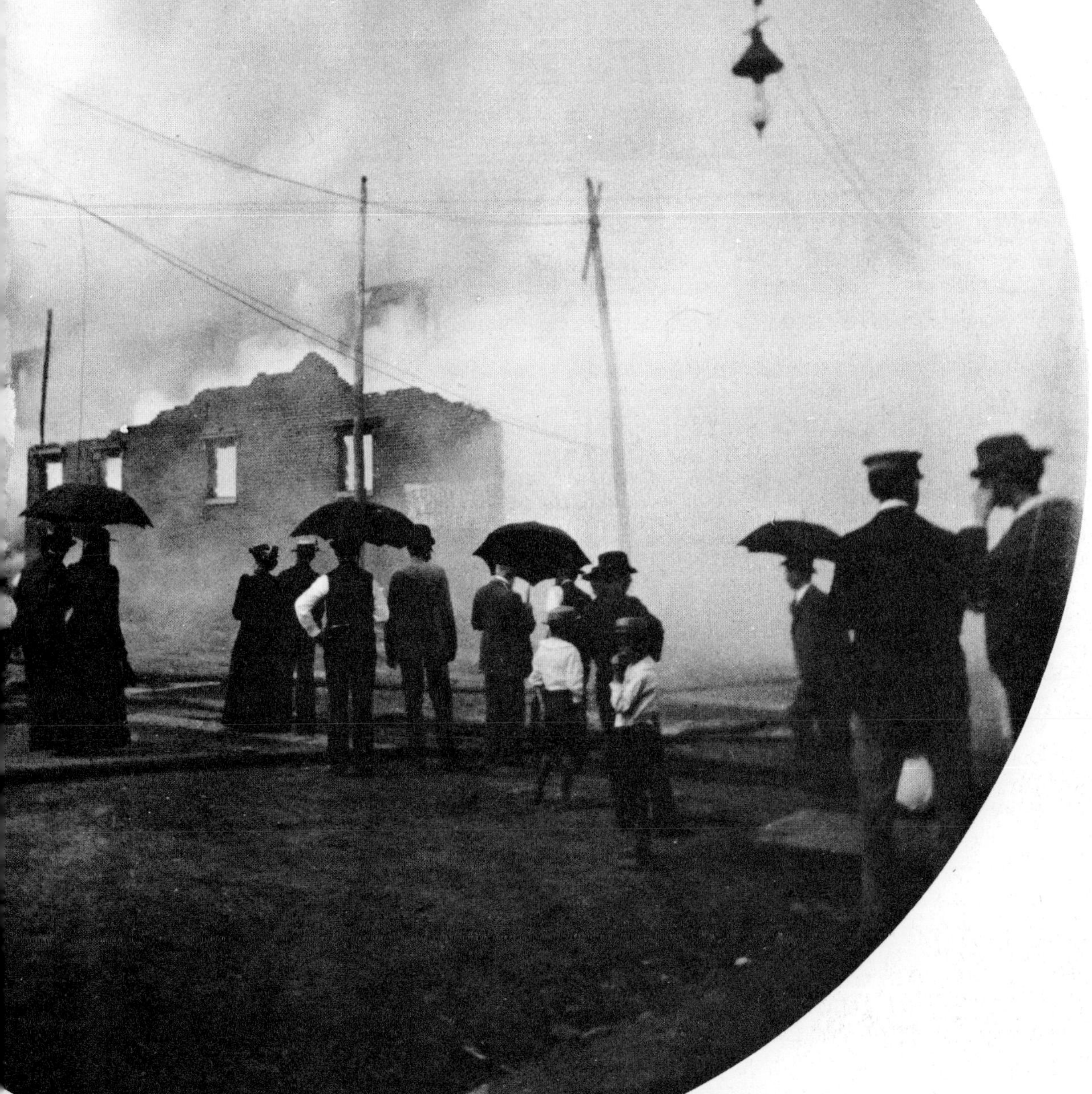

High water, like fire, was promptly memorialized by town photographers. With communities along the Ohio River among the most flood-prone in the nation, pictures such as this one (once in the files of the Illinois Central Railroad) were distressingly common. The locomotive stands in splendid isolation in the I.C.'s yards in Paducah, Kentucky, during the flood of 1913. Three decades later, the TVA tamed the Tennessee River, which empties into the Ohio at Paducah, and helped to reduce the flood menace.

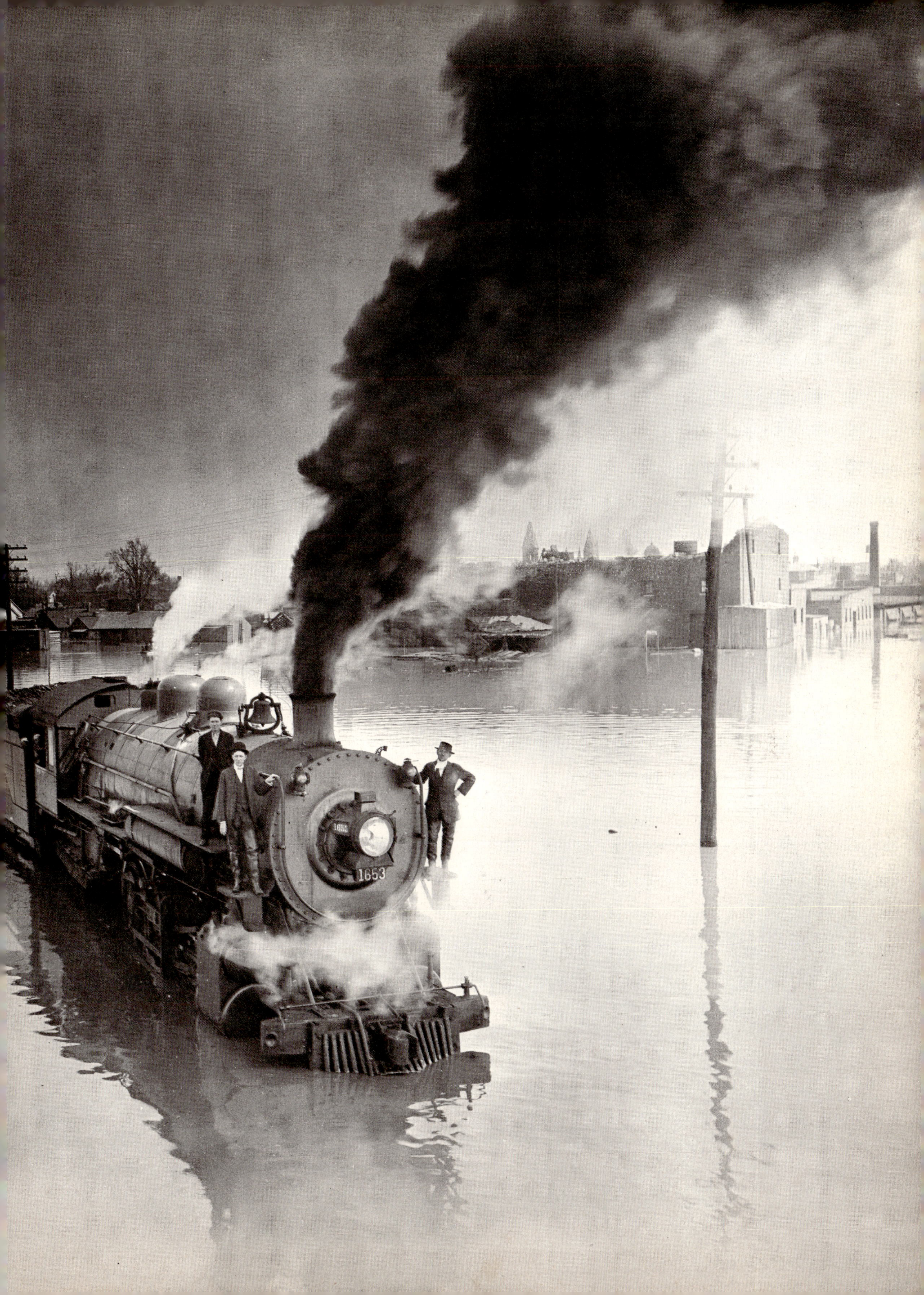
1653

COLLECTION OF AL FRED DANIEL

When Town Creek in Jackson, Mississippi, spilled over its banks in March of 1914, Albert Fred Daniel hauled his panoramic Cirkut camera to the roof of the Capitol Street building that housed his studio and made the view reproduced above. (The seemingly curved street is a distortion caused by the camera's panoramic sweep.) The throngs of flood-watchers included "hundreds of ladies" who observed "with keen interest the rise of the waters," according to the Jackson *Clarion-Ledger*. In the enlarged detail the boardinghouse proprietor gazes with classic resignation at her charges, who were among "any number of small boys" that *Clarion-Ledger* reporters found wading everywhere with obvious delight. After the floodwaters receded, Oscar Lamb Sales (left) was found to be dangerously undermined, and the movie house in the Heidelberg building (far left), which was featuring a watery epic about the loss of the *Titanic*, reported its organ and all its seats ruined. What damage, if any, was caused by the ominous twister at right is unknown. The threatened village in the picture, taken by Clinton Johnson in 1895, was in North Dakota.

212

LIBRARY OF CONGRESS

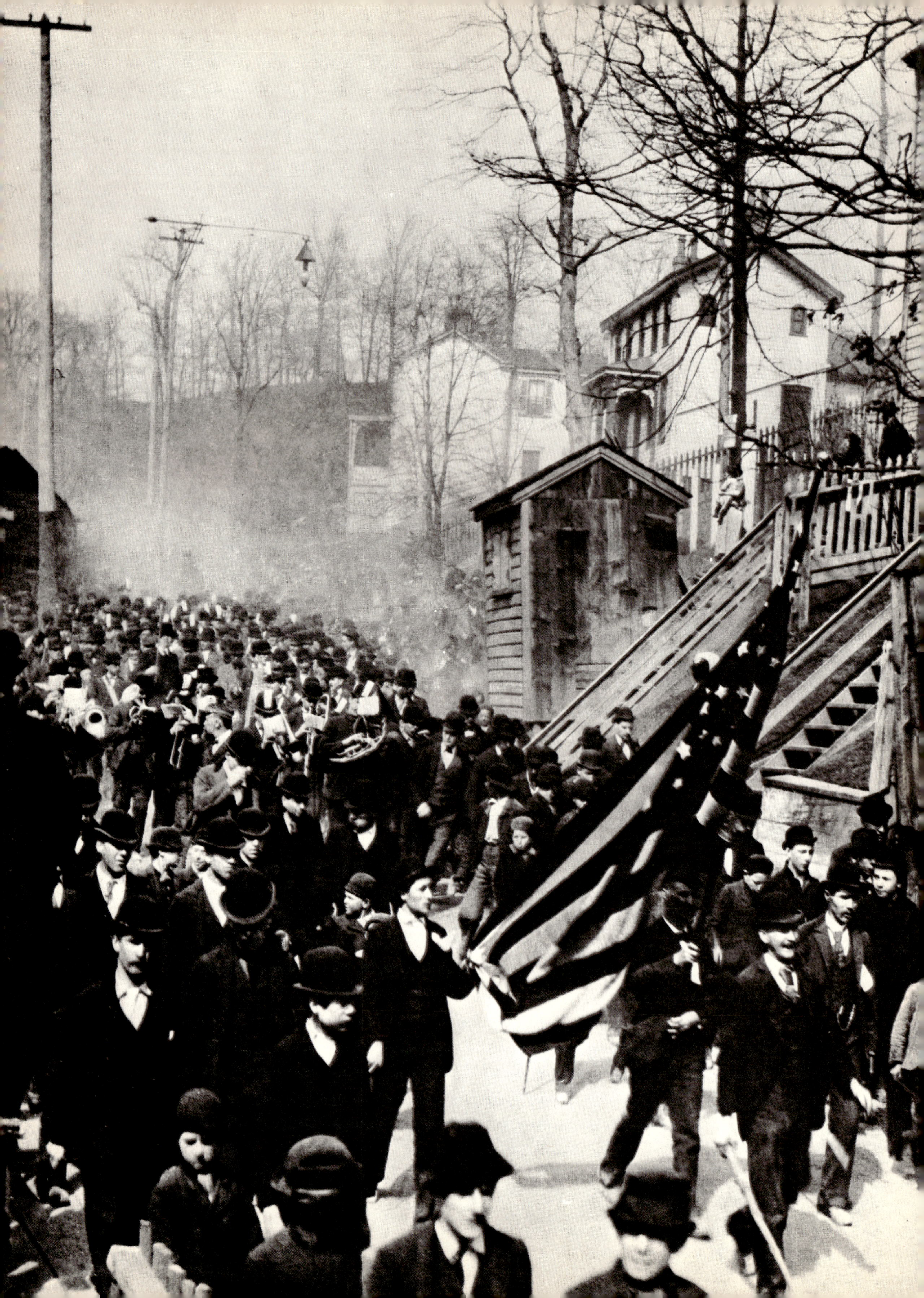

The 1890's was a tumultuous decade, economically and politically, with new forces rising up across the nation. Labor-management clashes grew in bitterness and violence. In July, 1892, the little town of Wallace, Idaho, was borne down under the weight of martial law after six died in pitched battles in the Coeur d'Alene mining region; federal troops were paraded through Wallace (below) to demonstrate the take-over. Two years later a force of a very different sort, Jacob Coxey's rag-tag Commonweal Army, marched from Coxey's hometown of Massillon, Ohio, to Washington to demand aid for the masses of unemployed. His "troops" are shown at left trailing through an unidentified Pennsylvania town, heartened by a brass band and accompanied by nearly every small boy in the county. In Washington the army melted away into ineffectualness and Coxey was arrested at the Capitol and jailed for walking on the grass.

OVERLEAF: More small-towners glimpsed the champion of the Democracy, William Jennings Bryan, than any previous national candidate. A magnetic, tireless campaigner, the Great Commoner is shown speaking for silver and against the trusts in Telluride, Colorado, in October, 1902. "He was in good voice and has lost none of his old power," a reporter wrote of Bryan's Colorado tour. Dignitaries on the platform shield their eyes from the bright afternoon sun.

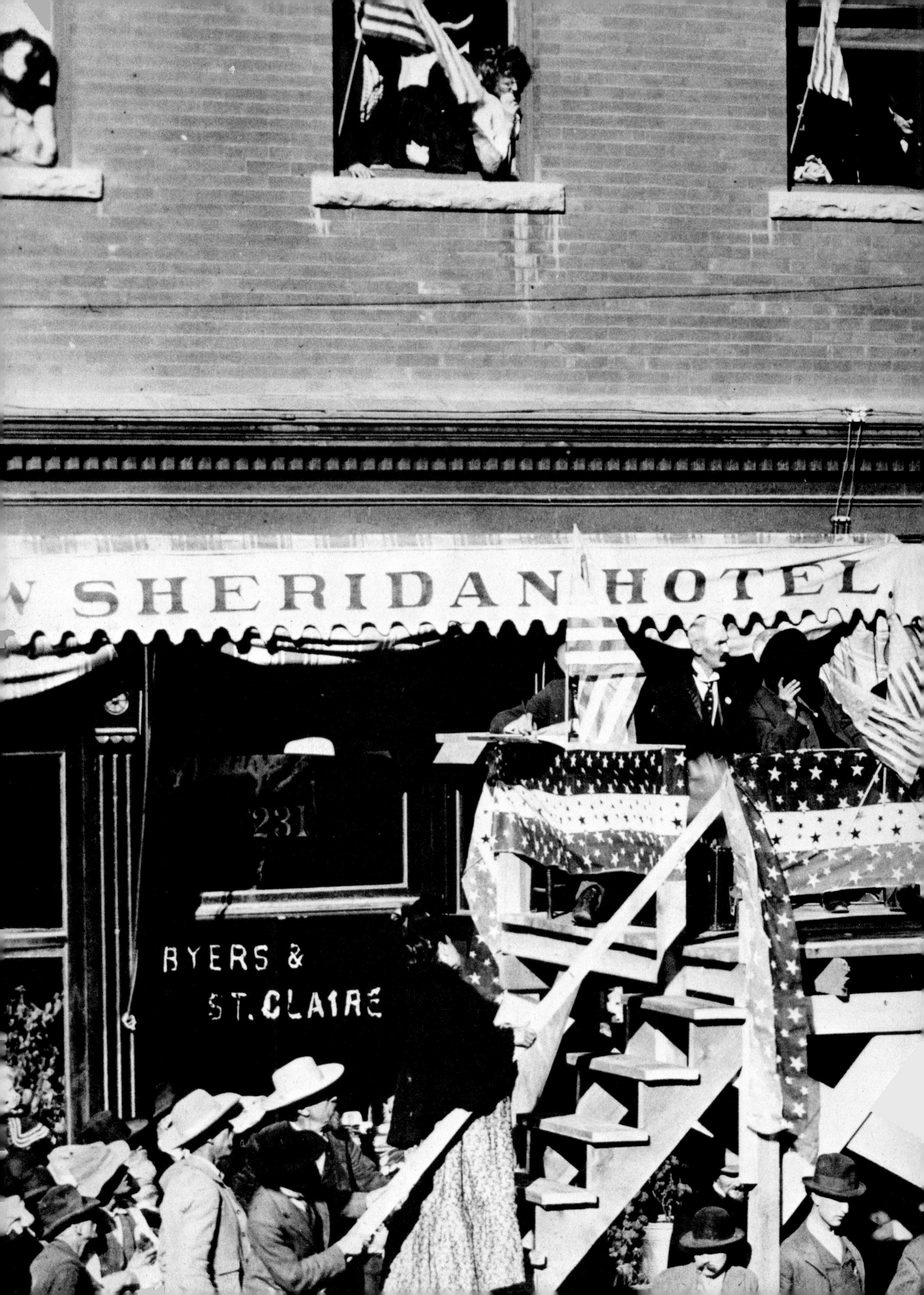

SHERIDAN HOTEL
231
BYERS &
ST. CLAIRE

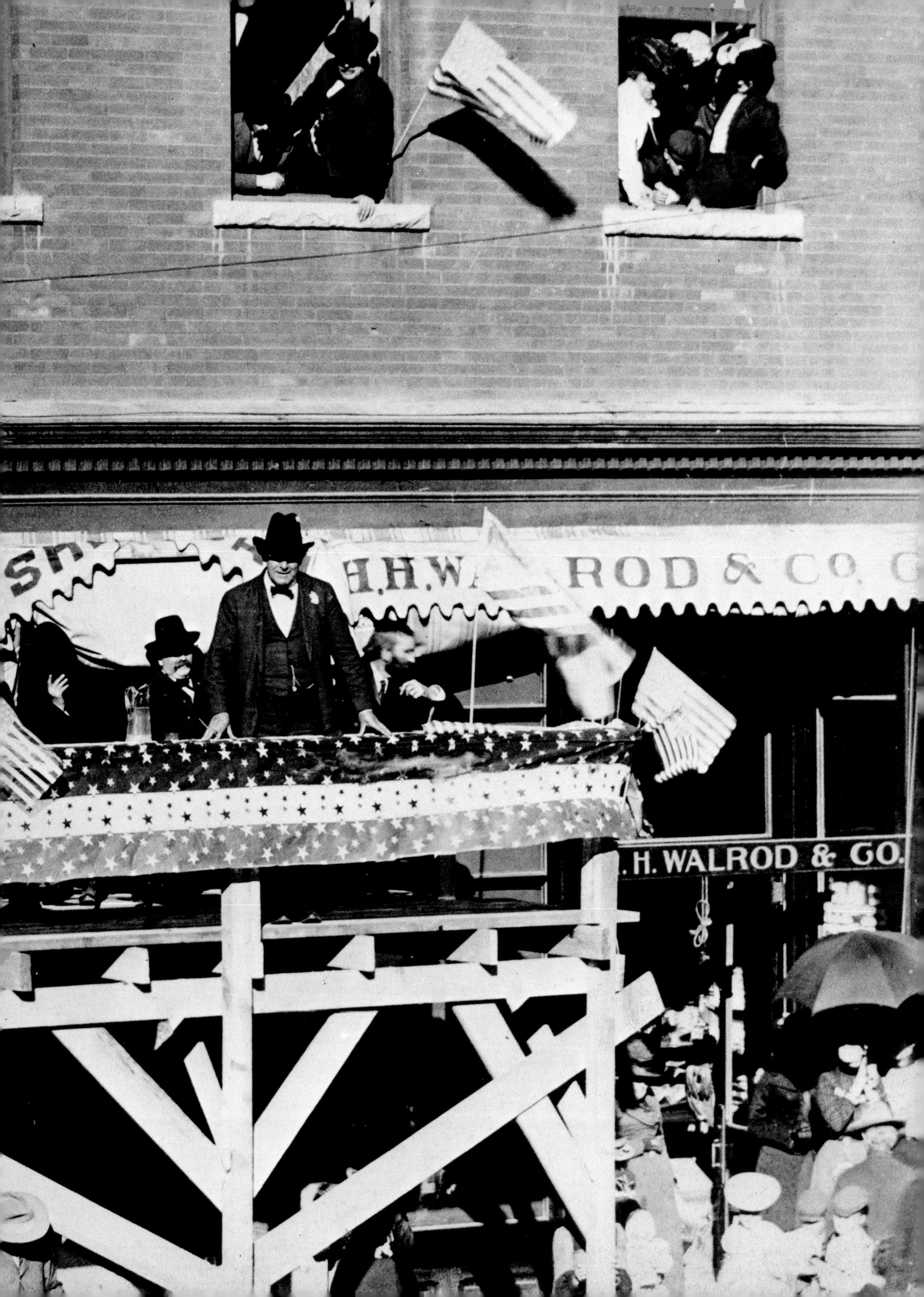

H.H.W ROD & CO.
H. WALROD & CO.

CHARLES PHELPS CUSHING

In 1910, in the spirit of boosterism and good fellowship, the businessmen of Hutchinson, Kansas, welcomed a visiting delegation of the Benevolent and Protective Order of Elks with the impressive display pictured above. The proprietor of the Taylor Motor Co., a Ford dealership, furnished most of the parade vehicles. At right is a unique, dazzling example of boosterism, the famous Corn Palace in Mitchell, South Dakota. Thousands of bushels of corn and tons of bundled oats and other grains went into the mosaic that decorated the palace in celebration of the 1907 harvest— 28 years before the Nazis corrupted the swastika and its ancient cosmic and religious symbolism. F. Elton Hill took the photograph.

218

LIBRARY OF CONGRESS

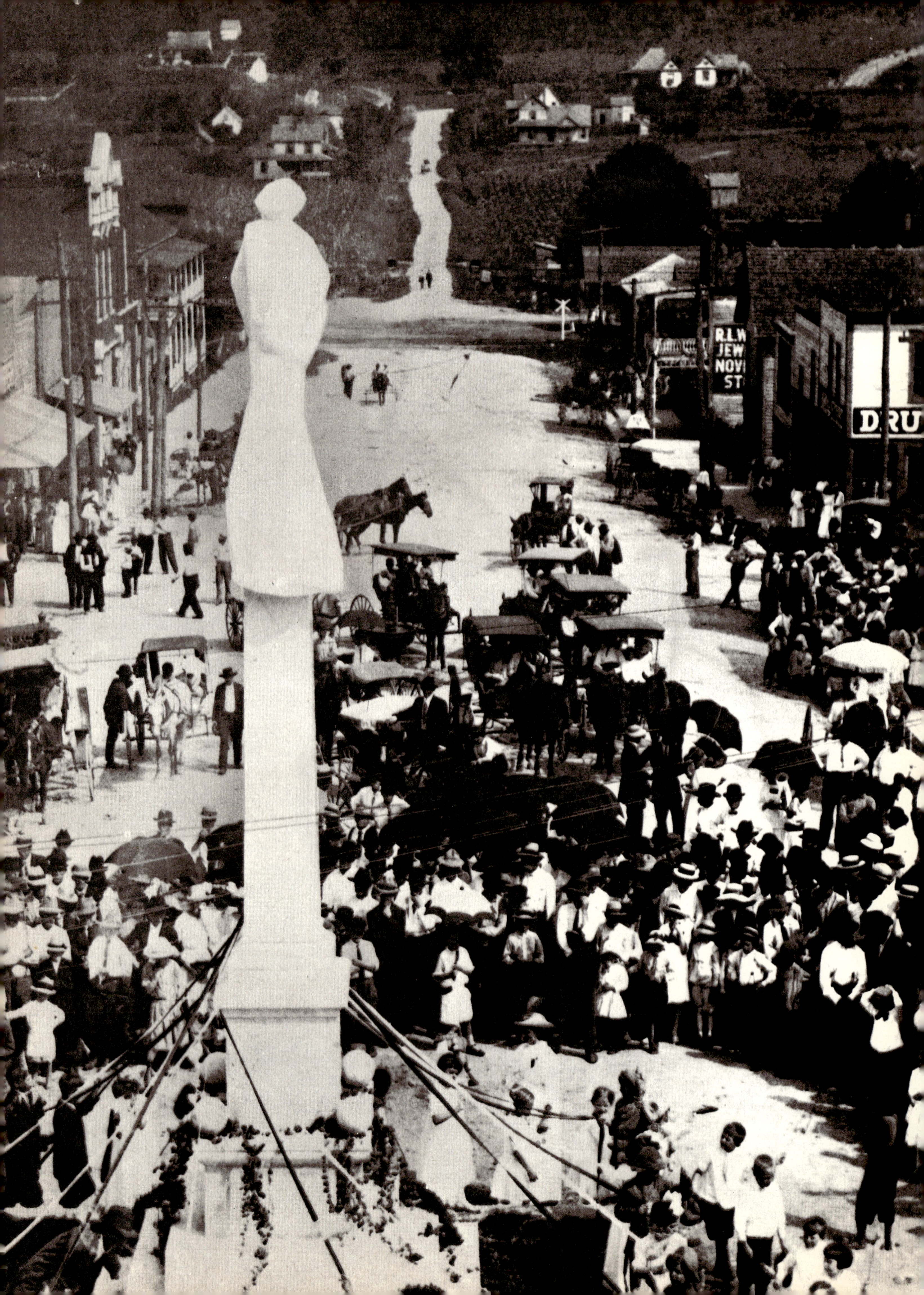
R.L.W
JEW
NOVI
ST
DRU

One of the strongest and most enduring characteristics of small-town life in the turn-of-the-century era was pride—pride in country, pride in local and national traditions. This was, to repeat Henry Seidel Canby's observation, a time when we were confident we knew what it meant to be Americans. The hatreds and bitter divisions of the Civil War had faded into shared legends of heroism by the boys in blue and gray. Opposite is First Street in Fort Payne, Alabama, on August 2, 1913, the occasion of the dedication of DeKalb County's Confederate monument. The whole town turned out for speechmaking and picnicing in the grove at Hawkins' Springs, followed by a grand march to the monument and the dramatic unveiling of the figure of the Confederate soldier by the youngsters in the foreground. It was a great day in Fort Payne's history, memorable for its "oratorical splendor" and "colorful pageantry." The patriotic celebrations that followed Admiral Dewey's gaudy victory over the Spanish fleet in Manila Bay in 1898 were nationwide. Below is Miller's restaurant (ham plate a dime, half a chicken for a quarter) in Massillon, Ohio, on Dewey Day. "Don't We" is spelled out in miniature flags; where is the rest of the punning play on words?

OVERLEAF: In 1907 Cooperstown, New York, was a century old, and Putt Telfer's photograph of the centennial observance was taken as a national guard regiment paraded down Main Street. It was a prideful day of flags and bunting, straw boaters and white dresses—a good day indeed to be alive.

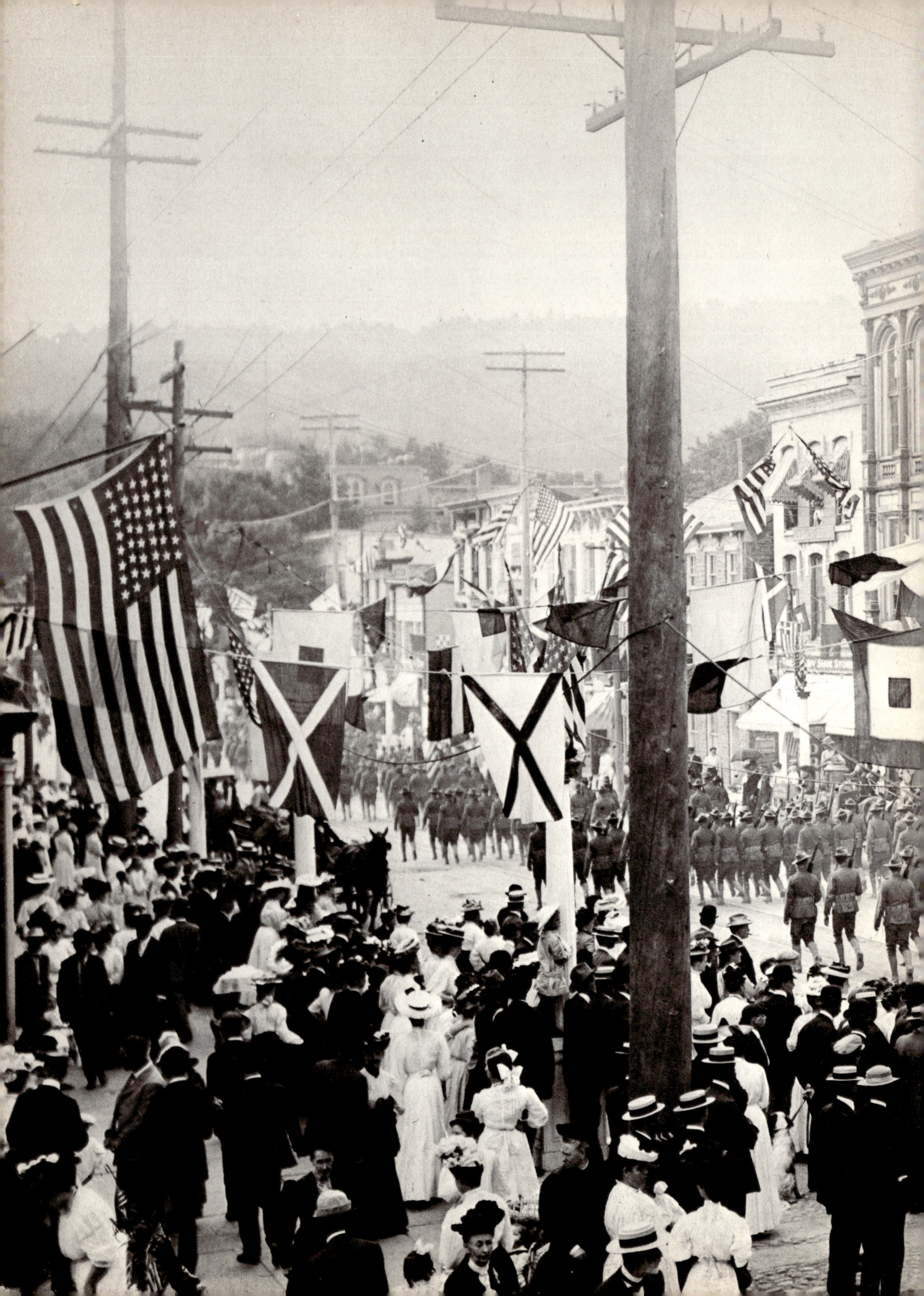

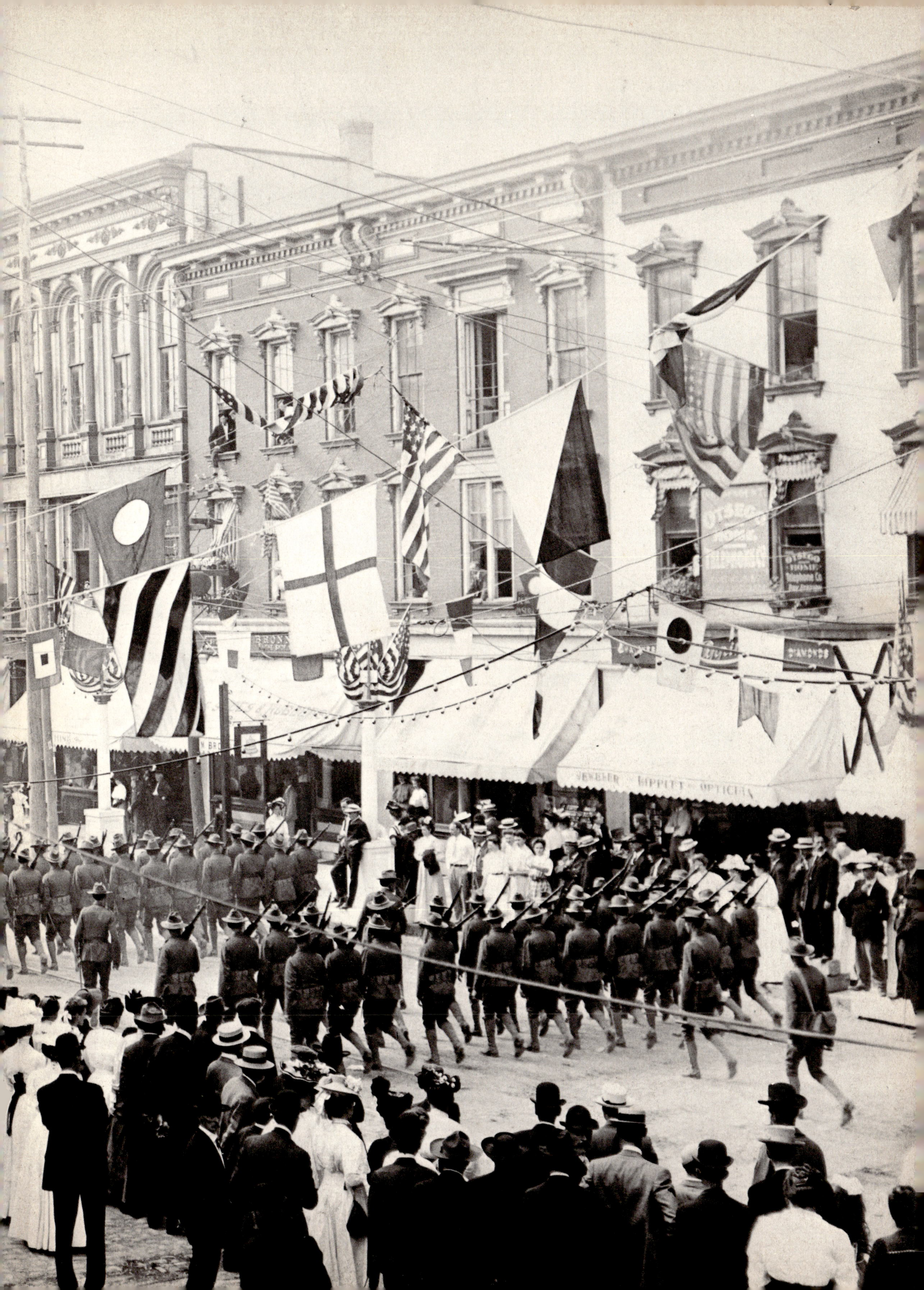
DIAMONDS